BAND DIRECTOR'S SURVIVAL GUIDE:

BAND DIRECTOR'S SURVIVAL GUIDE:

Planning and Conducting the Successful School Band Program

Eldon A. Janzen
Professor of Music
Director of Bands
University of Arkansas

Parker Publishing Company, Inc.
West Nyack, New York

Library of Congress Cataloging-in-Publication Data

Janzen, Eldon.
    Band director's survival guide.

    Bibliography: p.
    Includes index.
    1. Bands (Music)—Instruction and study.
2. School music—Instruction and study.   I. Title.
MT733.J36 1985   785.1'2'0712   85-9586

ISBN 0-13-056912-7
#12104523

ABOUT THE AUTHOR

Eldon Janzen has been Director of Bands at the University of Arkansas since 1970. In addition to serving as Director of the marching band and conductor of the symphonic band, he teaches instrumental methods and conducting at both the graduate and undergraduate levels.

Professor Janzen received his Bachelor of Music Education degree at Oklahoma State University and his Master of Music Education degree from North Texas State University, where he also served as Assistant to the Director of Bands.

Mr. Janzen taught in the public schools of Oklahoma and Texas for fourteen years before he was appointed Director of Music Activities for the Irving, Texas schools. His experience includes every facet of teaching and conducting bands, ranging from a small rural school to a large high school of 3,200 students. As Director of Music Activities, he guided the classroom music programs of 19 elementary schools and all the band and choral activities of six secondary schools, involving a total of 25,000 students.

During this time, Mr. Janzen developed band programs which consistently produced outstanding performing organizations in both marching and concert competition. He is frequently invited to serve as clinician, guest conductor, and adjudicator at such contests as Six Flags, Worlds of Music, Tri-State of Enid, Oklahoma, and many others. His professional affiliations include American Bandmasters Association, Music Educators National Conference, Kappa Kappa Psi, and Lions International. Mr. Janzen has served as president of both the Texas and Arkansas Bandmaster's Associations and is currently president of the Southwest Division of College Band Directors National Association.

ABOUT THIS BOOK

Written for the band director, *Band Director's Survival Guide* presents techniques and teaching strategies that have been used in actual teaching situations ranging from the smallest rural school to a well-organized suburban school system of more than 25,000 students. These techniques and strategies reflect current trends and practices in some of the most progressive instrumental music systems in the country and serve as a checklist for every teacher who continues to evaluate his or her role as a school band director.

This book focuses on your most critical and common problems as a band director, such as·

- What do I tell students, parents, and staff when they want to know the purposes of a school band (Chapter 1)?
- How can I plan a budget even when I have no money to spend (Chapter 2)?
- When selecting students for the band, how do I find and interest the right ones (Chapter 3)?
- What clues do I look for in a student who may be planning to drop out of the band program (Chapter 4)?
- How do I select the appropriate teaching materials for my beginning students (Chapter 5)?
- How can I relate goals, achievement, and discipline to learning (Chapter 6)?
- How do I train students to listen for and hear correct ensemble structure (Chapter 7)?
- How do I teach breathing for better quality and attack in the concert band (Chapter 8)?
- How do I teach students to play in tune (Chapter 9)?

- How can I expose my students to a variety of musical styles (Chapter 10)?

- How can I assess the strengths and weaknesses of a performance (Chapter 11)?

- How can I communicate with my students in "marching language" (Chapter 12)?

- How do I select students for the stage band (Chapter 13)?

- How can I gain outside support from parents (Chapter 14)?

Many forms and musical samples are included to help you plan and conduct the school band program. For example, the "Music Summary Sheet" helps you plan a typical marching performance regardless of what style the band may use. In addition, four formations are provided on a scale drawing of a football field to further help you plan your marching program.

Seating charts are given to show you the best instrument positions for maximum sound, and sample music class schedules help you arrange the school day when there are one, two, or three director/teachers available.

In short, *Band Director's Survival Guide* offers you detailed guidelines for building a total band program. It's a book you should have handy every day, all year 'round.

Eldon Janzen

Contents

1

The Role
of the Band Director
in Music Education

It would be interesting to note the number of band directors in the teaching profession today who arrived at their present status by design, as opposed to those who drifted in through less-structured avenues. Many present-day band directors accepted a position in the public schools as a secondary, rather than a primary option. Such people candidly admit to other aspirations in the field of professional music. Most often the original motivation was in an area of performance which gave way early to the more regular and predictable life in the public schools.

ASSESSING MOTIVES AND DEFINING THE MISSION IN TEACHING

The teachers who originally intended to perform, as well as those who planned a scheduled entry into the band field, shared at some time a certain vague and nebulous comprehension of the role and scope of the band director. Such a lack of understanding is often

1

the honest product of the college curriculum in music where the emphasis is placed on how to play, rather than how to teach. The entire learning process emphasizes (and often justifiably so) the act of acquiring, rather than disseminating, information or skills.

The role of that person whose special mission in life is to influence behavior and teach musical skills must be defined at some point. Sustaining a career in music education requires the adaptability to accept a certain role and authority in the school and community. This process is often difficult. It is foreign to the personality of many of us to be viewed as the one person in a community who is expected to know everything about music, band, behavior and discipline, and all related matters. Such an expansive job description has been self-imposed by the profession. The multiple skills needed for planning, teaching, and conducting bands in music programs of excellence are common, and as a result, expected.

CHARACTERISTICS OF THE SUCCESSFUL TEACHER

Thus far, professional educators have been largely ineffective in predicting exactly who can successfully assume the role of a good teacher and music authority, but at some point in their career, he or she should develop the following traits:

1. Discipline of self in order to clearly define priorities and objectives. Simply stated, this trait means knowing what the mission is, finding out how to get it done, and being willing to sacrifice the hours within the framework of a rigid schedule to complete the task.

2. An understanding of human behavior which provides the insight needed to motivate others to the achievement of a goal or an objective. One need not necessarily view himself as a leader; often people who stimulate or motivate very well see themselves as nonleaders, but they universally attain communicative skills and have an intense interest in sharing knowledge and skills with others.

3. A substantial knowledge of, and interest in, the music ensemble which leads to the skill of listening to sound in terms of structure and quality. This trait encompasses the entire realm of making beautiful music: pitch, rhythm, phrasing, dynamics, and all of the other qualities of a credible performance of any and all ensembles. We are talking now about the

sometimes innate ability to know how to go about creating a work of art. This is the final measure of the conductor/teacher.

The first two traits listed can and do apply to many other fields of endeavor and are almost universally in demand. Only the third trait sets the band director apart among the successful in his chosen field. Devotion to this ideal is ultimately the reason for the overwhelming success which keeps such an individual firmly entrenched in the profession of teaching and conducting musical ensembles.

DEVELOPING A PHILOSOPHY OF MUSIC EDUCATION

The classical concept of a "philosophy" is sometimes hard to understand and even more difficult to explain. The great philosophers in history laid the groundwork for the present course in education, but we are perhaps even more indebted to those who determined that music had an important place in the curriculum of the public schools. While the real thrust of the band movement in America did not begin until after World War II, the development which began before the turn of the century was already sounding the trumpet for the massive infusion of band instrument instruction that was to come. Even after the close of World War I, the stage was being set for what would be the giant of the "extracurricular" world, succeeding against all the odds to compete with virtually everything in the established school curriculum.

TEACHING IN THE AGE OF ACCOUNTABILITY

In the years since 1946, the band program, with its army of supporting patrons and parents, has evolved almost full cycle into an era where it must submit to the eye of scrutiny and answer the hard questions of justification and accountability which the tax-paying public is demanding of its schools.

Band directors across the land are being asked to review their budget requests and reappraise their most important priorities. The clear message is that reduced funding is now a reality, and even that condition may be a luxury compared to programs in major metropolitan schools whose very existence is threatened.

Most teachers will be forced to take a hard look at the support level for the band program; supporting a band is expensive. Confidence in the true worth of the program will be put to the test.

Respect for values and support were once taken for granted, and the funding at adequate levels was routine; however, today's director of bands will find his or her mission is much more than the perpetuation of basic skills to others. Administrative officers—principals and school superintendents—no longer operate with independence and authority over budgetary or policy matters. The many "kinsmen" of the "three R's" which have become fused into education now also demand a slice of the pie making it constantly more difficult to protect general budgets for music and the arts.

DISCIPLINE AND INDIVIDUAL RIGHTS

Matters of policy in discipline and program objectives seldom went beyond the level of the superintendent in the past. The political revolution of individual rights since 1960 has completely revised the authority role of the public school teacher. Today we find school board members eagerly injecting themselves into what was once a private realm of policy in matters of grading, attendance, extra rehearsal, travel, contest participation, etc. Parents in disagreement with a band director's decision no longer resolve the conflict in the director's office or that of his principal; too often this conference is just a rest stop on the way to a meeting of the full board of school trustees. Thus we have witnessed the erosion of the school administrator's role as final authority and with it a treasured alliance which often developed between his administration and his faculty.

Instrumental music programs will survive and continue in good health, but the skills of those who direct them must grow to meet the challenge as in any changing society. The bandmaster of the 80's and beyond will constantly become more skilled in human relations as well as maintaining the basic techniques of the art. He will become a more articulate spokesman for the combination of music and youth, and at the same time become more effective in translating the art for adults. Unfortunately, the technique of teaching music through the medium of the band continues, in far too many band rooms, to be a side effect of music education instead of the central purpose, and this situation must improve.

THE IMPORTANCE OF COMMITMENT IN EDUCATION

For the teacher, the love of music must develop into a commitment, a deep and total conviction of the "rightness" of teaching musical skills to others, and the urgency to share with others this universal art of communication which needs no interpreter. The strength of such a commitment may develop very gradually within the years of success and failure that trace every career. The important and abiding difference for those who stay the course is that the success, regardless of how minimal at the outset, continues to wield a far greater influence on professional commitment than the manifold failures. A lone and small victory in a year of teaching gilds the tarnish of a score of failures. The gradual multiplying reinforcement of small successes is the elemental process by which commitment grows strong.

ARTICULATING A PHILOSOPHY OF CULTURAL ENRICHMENT AND COMMUNITY SERVICE

The art of capsulizing a "philosophical vitamin" is a tradition usually consisting of a reassuring maxim, saying, bible verse, or "golden rule." Adopting such an axiom is a good first step; its therapeutic balm can be called upon at will, and it can be developed, or even reconstructed, to match the maturity of the commitment.

For example, a statement such as the following can provide a good beginning which is easily articulated into conversational terms:

> *Music education is for the cultural and moral enrichment of the student in the public schools. A valuable outgrowth of the program is the development of organizations which render outstanding school and community service.*

Who would debate the direction of a music program so described? No one is arguing that the hard core of academic subjects is not important, even paramount if you must, but who would deny the need for culture in our society? What patron wants his child to pass the way of academia without the opportunity to nurture the very soul of life?

The statement makes an honest concession to community service. Bands must play for people; a performance unheard by others has lost the power of communication. Will the kinds of performances required by bands upset the concept of the musical mission? Let us not fall prey to that false virtue. The band is the most versatile ensemble of this or any other century. The sophisticated mobile outdoor musical units we once called "marching bands" are now combining the finest literature written with the most artistic and skillful flow of pattern and movement ever seen, in addition to all of the traditional functions upon which its reputation was built. Concert bands can emulate and authentically recreate every known musical style and revel in an evergrowing library of literature written exclusively for this medium. The band as an ensemble has no limits; only its leadership occasionally falls into myopic entrenchment.

BIBLIOGRAPHY

Dewey, John. *Experiences in Education.* (New York: MacMillan, 1938)

Hoffer, Charles. *Teaching Music in the Secondary School.* (Menlo Park, CA: Addison-Wesley, 1969)

House, Robert William. *Instrumental Music for Today's Schools.* (Englewood Cliffs, NJ: Prentice-Hall, 1965)

Jones, Llewellyn Bruce. *Building the Instrumental Music Department.* (Chicago: Carl Fischer, 1949)

Prescott, Gerald R., and M. A. Prescott. *Getting Results with School Bands.* (Published jointly by Carl Fischer, Chicago, and Paul A. Schmitt Music Co., Minneapolis, 1938)

Snyder, Keith D. *School Music Administration and Supervision,* second ed. (Boston: Allyn & Bacon, 1965)

2

Budget Planning
and Administration of
the Band Program

Assessment of the planning and administration of a total band program is a comprehensive task. The information in this chapter deals with those acts which are normally required of the person in charge of a school band program employing one to three director/ teachers whose students eventually progress into one high school. This situation can include the possibility of several grade schools and one or more middle or junior high schools. Under these circumstances the band director in charge is responsible to, and must depend upon, an immediate superior (principal or superintendent) for the following areas of planning and decisions:

1. Assignment of teaching duties
2. Scheduling of class-rehearsal times and location
3. Approval of performances and travel
4. Processing of requests for expenditures and purchases

ASSIGNMENT OF TEACHING DUTIES AND SCHEDULES

There seems to be no standardized guideline for the teaching load of a band director. In the small- and medium-sized school system, it is generally a pragmatic matter of scheduling a rehearsal period for the main performing group and utilizing the remainder of the day to meet beginners and possibly a secondary group. The band director who has a principal sympathetic to the diverse needs of the total band program is most fortunate. Such an administrator recognizes that a teaching assignment in band cannot be equated with that of the English or Mathematics teacher.

Compromises in freedom during the regularly scheduled teaching day must be made in exchange for the time before and after school which is spent in section rehearsals, athletic service, and other activities. Some schools occasionally require teaching service in academic or supervisory (study hall) areas. Such conditions must be accepted until the band director can prove that his specialized skills are not being efficiently utilized outside the area of band-related teaching.

Figure 2-1 shows some typical schedule arrangements for the small band staff.

One Director/Teacher System

Period	Activity/Assignment
Pre-school	Section/individual teaching
1st	Full band, high school; usually utilizing the pre-school period in preparation for marching and concert events
2nd	Preparation/travel period to junior high or elementary schools
3rd	Beginning woodwinds
Lunch	Beginning percussion
4th	Beginning brass
5th	Intermediate/remedial group
6th	Full band, junior high school
After School:	Section/individual teaching

Figure 2-1 Sample schedule arrangements.

Two Director/Teacher System

Period	High School Activity	Jr. High/Middle School Activity
Pre-School	Director "A" and "B": Full band	-----
1st	Full band, continued	-----
2nd	Director "B": "Second" Band	Director "A": Beginning percussion
3rd	-----	Director "A" and "B": Full band
Lunch	-----	Full band, continued
4th	-----	Director "A": Beginning clarinets; Director "B": Beginning flutes
5th	----	Director "A": Beginning saxophones; Director "B": Beginning horns
6th	Director "A": Stage Band	Director "B": Beginning low brasses
After School:	Section/individual teaching	

Three Director/Teacher System

Period	High School	Jr. High School	Middle School
Pre-School	Directors "A", "B", "C": Full band/ sectionals	-----	-----
1st	Full band, continued	-----	-----
2nd	Director "A": Music theory	Director "C": Intermediate band	Director "B": Beginning clarinets
3rd	Director "A": Planning/travel	Director "C": Beginning percussion	Director "B": Preparation/travel

Figure 2-1   *(continued)*

Three Director/Teacher System (continued)

Period	High School	Jr. High School	Middle School
Lunch	-----	Directors"A", "B", "C": Full band	-----
4th.	-----	Full band, continued	-----
5th.	-----	-----	Director "A": Beginning trumpets. Director "B": Beginning saxophones. Director "C": Beginning horns.
6th.	Director "A" Stage band	-----	Director "B": Beginning trombones. Director "C": Beginning low brasses.
After School:	Director "A": Section/ individual teaching	Director "B": Section/individual teaching	Director "C": Section/individual teaching

Figure 2-1 *(continued)*

Advantages of the "One Teacher" System

Many directors find themselves cast in the role of the "one teacher" band program. Such a role is difficult but not impossible, and it can produce excellent results. It has several advantages. Such a teaching environment makes it easier to develop continuity in the program since the teaching philosophy of only one person is represented. The problems of instructional coordination are minimal. Allegiance and loyalty to the band program by students is normally better because they grow accustomed to one teaching personality. The single teacher involved can speak for the total program in matters of budget and scheduling.

Team Teaching With Two or More Teachers

The school providing two or more teachers has some obvious advantages. It becomes important that teachers understand and utilize the benefits of "Team Teaching." Too often a second or third member of such a team finds it convenient to recede to an inert role, or retires to the teachers' lounge for coffee. This passivity destroys the concept of team effectiveness, particularly in the mind of the principal and the faculty. The presence of two or more teachers in the room during a full band rehearsal can be very effective. Their presence demands, first and foremost, an understanding that the conductor on the podium can be momentarily interrupted for external input and reinforcement by those in assistance. This reinforcement can take the form of agreement with what the conductor says, calling attention to a related point, or initiating the isolation of a problem. Team teaching can provide a helpful second or third opinion about important matters of sound and balance. Members of the team must feel comfortable about calling individuals out of the rehearsal for private help when it would result in an economy of time and effort, such as the need for instrument or reed adjustment and specialized help for a rhythmic or technical problem.

Further Advantages of Team Teaching

In addition to the advantages of team teaching, a second or third person provides individual and specialized teaching skills. Teachers with applied training specialities make up a more complete staff to cover woodwind, brass, and percussion areas. These teachers can also accept responsibilities in marching auxiliaries such as twirling and flag and rifle, and in arranging and drill design specialties.

The important aspect of multiple staffing is in *utilization*. Each member of such a team must feel comfortable in his or her role and must remain motivated to be constantly involved in the teaching process.

PERFORMANCE AND TRAVEL

The School Calendar

Administration of the school calendar is generally the responsibility of the principal. He must schedule certain events which are dictated by the superintendent and the school board. These events would include:

1. Beginning and closing dates of the school terms
2. School vacation periods such as Christmas and Easter and other religious holidays

3. Official government or national holidays to be observed by school personnel

4. In-service training, professional conferences, or teacher "work days" when students will be excused from class attendance

5. Days for parent visitation and conferences

6. Observance of special events related to community activities such as "Fair Days," "Centennial" or "Rodeo days," and other "special" days when school will be dismissed

7. The official schedule of football, basketball, tennis, volleyball, track, and other athletic events

8. Scheduled testing of all students such as SAT, ACT, or other tests of achievement

9. Competitive speech, drama, or other academic events

These are events which at some time or other will interrupt the normal sequence of band rehearsals and scheduled band activities. They are dates which will often require band participation. They must be considered when scheduling band concerts or travel to contests and festivals.

The Band Calendar

It is the obligation of the band director to assemble complete information about all events involving band participation, and to make them known to the principal at the earliest possible time at the begining of the school year. This calendar includes events in which band participation is taken for granted such as football and parade performances. Perhaps more important, however, are those specialized band events which administrators are less likely to remember or know about. These events include:

1. Auditions for district, regional, and all-state select bands.

2. Performances of select groups resulting from such auditions.

3. Solo and ensemble competitions.

4. Full-band marching competition. There is normally one event sponsored by the state educators' association each fall. Numerous "invitational" events may also be considered.

5 Full-band concert and sight-reading festival competition, usually sponsored by the state association at both a district or regional level as well as the state level for those who achieve a certain rating.

6. Full-band competition in late spring of an "invitational" nature including opportunities in Europe. These events are often scheduled in conjunction with amusement park facilities and trips to historically significant locales with valid educational opportunities.
7. Full-band concerts and assembly programs, usually two or three each school year.
8. Travel to other schools in the district for purposes of recruiting beginners. This may involve the full band or selected students.

The Director's Responsibility in Finalizing the Calendar

The foregoing list represents events which should be presented in written form for consideration and approval. A written response by an appropriate official should be requested and retained on file with assurance that the approved events are placed on the official school calendar. In conjunction with the request and approval of such events, a clear agreement about the cost and provision for paying such costs should be formalized. In many schools, the expense of events sponsored or sanctioned by a state educational association (including athletic service) are considered to be obligations of the school district. Other invitational and recreational events are funded with the help of outside sources or by the students on an individual basis. Regardless of the means for financing travel and participation, serious misunderstanding can be prevented by written requests which detail all aspects of performance and travel.

PLANNING A BUDGET: PROGRAM FUNDING

Two Purposes for Budget Planning

The preparation of a budget for a band program serves two important purposes. A carefully researched budget proposal: (1) assists in planning a year-long program of band activity and the financial support necessary to sustain it; and (2) informs yourself, your staff, your administration, and any outside support group about the band program in terms which are often more meaningful than other objective methods.

Administrative Resistance to Budgets

Some school administrators refuse to allocate specific sums of money to the support of any phase of the music program. This condition has several explanations:

1. The given school district has very limited funds available for maintenance and operation for all phases of instruction and consequently spends very little on the band program; adequate funding of the band program must come from other sources such as band parents organizations.

2. The school district depends heavily upon unpredictable sources of funding such as that provided by the federal government or private industry. Exact information for financial support of the school may not be readily available and the administrator prefers to deal with funding the band program after other priorities are taken care of.

3. The financing of the school district is such that all reasonable expenditures in every area can be accommodated and the superintendent does not anticipate any difficulty in meeting funding requests.

4. The superintendent does not wish to be committed to any specific level of financial support for the program, preferring to deal with each request on an individual basis. Needs can be funded if resources are available at the time; otherwise they must wait for a more favorable financial climate. This procedure tends to deal with financial needs on a first-come, first-served basis and frequently contributes to the theory that the "wheel which squeaks the loudest, gets oiled first!"

None of the above reasons reflect good fiscal-management practice and should not serve to deter the band director from researching and preparing an annual budget. In many respects it becomes even more important to plan a thorough budget when financial support is uncertain. Under these conditions, the director is forced to make some important evaluative decisions to place the years' activities which depend on money in priority order. Such uncertainty of funding can serve to encourage more active support from band parents or booster groups. The director may even want to schedule a business-like discussion of his projected budget with the principal or superintendent. Such a discussion, when properly approached, can help an administrator realize he is dealing with a music person who has a grasp of financial matters and is planning to administer the spending of even meager funds in a wise and **prudent** manner. It can lead to the establishment of a budget allocation in future years.

Fortunately, most competent administrators will solicit and honor the customary process of budget planning and preparation. In such a condition of employment the band director must be willing to devote the time and effort to adequately prepare a budget document which correctly reflects the needs and costs of the program.

It can be helpful to recognize that there are varying degrees of financial support in the public schools. Such general conditions are described in the following four kinds of budgets and these can be helpful in establishing budgetary priorities and levels of spending:

Budget Types

1. *Absolute.* A budget which provides the minimum needs required to meet classes regularly and provides a minimum program of instruction and performing activity. Such a budget would insure the "status quo" and discourage normal growth and progress. It would depend heavily on outside support for incentives such as trips and awards.

2. *Adequate.* The budget has provisions for ample facilities, equipment, supplies, and services, including instructional support for the normal growth and development of the band program. This budget represents a generally conservative and prudent approach to funding but includes assurance that justified needs will be met.

3. *Ambitious.* This budget provides for ample service, supplies, equipment, and the expansion of facilities to encourage growth and development. Personnel may be added to assist in development in advance of the actual need.

4. *Luxury.* The limits of financial aid are of no concern. In addition to the features listed before, added ways to supplement and support the program can be explored. Such programs are supported by an industrial tax base which must be expended each tax year. The band director in such a program would be able to fully finance year-end trips without extra fund-raising effort. Instruments and equipment are often provided at no expense to the student. Luxurious rehearsal

and performance facilities are provided. Consultants and specialists assist with all aspects of the program. Convention attendance, routine travel, and other expenses for the teaching staff are subsidized.

BUDGET PREPARATION

A budget projection or request is normally done for a twelve-month period covering the fiscal year rather than the calendar year. The fiscal year usually corresponds more closely to the school year, from July 1 to June 30 of the following year.

Items Not Included in Band Budgets

Certain kinds of expenditures are not determined by the band director and consequently are not a part of his budget-preparation procedure. These expenditures would include staff salaries, utility expenses, and maintenance to the building or rehearsal facilities. New equipment such as tubas, oboes, or sound and recording equipment is regarded as "capital outlay." As capital outlay, it may be bought with funds generated through bonded indebtedness and must be repaid, with interest, over a long period of time amounting to 20 years or more. Administrators are extremely reluctant to purchase instruments with this kind of money since the equipment often becomes obsolete before the bond debt is repaid. Some school districts make a distinction between "replacement" equipment and "new" or added equipment. Tax revenues which are generated on an annual basis may then be spent for replacing worn-out equipment as opposed to that which expands the inventory. Under such guidelines, new-equipment requests would be submitted separately for consideration; these would include requests for uniforms since the usable life is seldom more than ten years. An effort is normally made to purchase such items from special allocations.

Routine Budget Items

A list of items which would appear on most band budgets is found in Figure 2-2. The preparation of such a budget is a somewhat tedious chore but should be done carefully. Many sources of information will be consulted in compiling accurate projections. Bear in mind that once the figures are submitted and approved they are somewhat binding. Administrators do not like to deal with requests for frequent

Budget Request
Band Department
Central High School
Date

Services
   1. Instrument repair   _____
   2. Office equipment repair   _____
   3. Video and audio equipment repair   _____
   4. Piano tuning   _____

                 Total   _____

Supplies
   1. Office, photocopy, and recording   _____
   2. Music manuscript and folders   _____
   3. Marble dust, paint for field marking   _____
   4. Reeds, springs, oil, pads, corks, minor
      repairs   _____

                 Total   _____

Replacement equipment
   1. Permanent inventory   _____
   2. Expendable: Percussion head, sticks,
      flags, poles, etc.   _____
   3. Uniforms   _____
   4. Office and furniture, music stands   _____
   5. Sound and recording   _____

                 Total   _____

Travel
   1. Transportation   _____
   2. Meals   _____
   3. Lodging   _____

                 Total   _____

Filming and recording
   1. Marching contest   _____
   2. Playing contest   _____
   3. Record production   _____

                 Total   _____

Entry fees
   1. Region, all-state, solo, and ensemble   _____
   2. Organizational   _____

                 Total   _____

Music
   1. Football and marching   _____
   2. Concert and contest   _____
   3. Teaching materials   _____
   4. Solo and ensemble   _____
   5. Stage band   _____

                 Total   _____
         GRAND TOTAL   _____

Figure 2-2   Example of budget request.

revisions and changes, especially when it requires more money. It is not wise for the director to protect his lack of ability to project an accurate budget with inflated figures. This practice tends to reduce the administration's confidence in the professional advice of such a person. It is much better to be armed with current catalogs, price lists, and discount information in order to present the most accurate and up-to-date projection available.

Music dealers and instrument repairmen can be quite helpful in assisting with the preparation of a repair budget or instrument replacement request. In requesting the purchase of items costing more than $250 it is wise to stipulate that competitive bids be solicited. Such procedures are usually handled by the business office of a school but can also be solicited by the band director. It is most convenient and tempting to buy equipment from a favorite dealer, but considerable savings can be effected through the competitive-bid process. This process usually results in a favorite dealer also becoming a low bidder if he values other facets of the school's business.

The matter of competitive bids on repair work is not quite as easily accomplished since accurate appraisals are difficult to make on all but a complete overhaul of a given instrument. Much of the year's repair work will be of a minor or minimum nature usually referred to as "PC" or playing-condition repair. In such cases the director should take the repairman's recommendation on what can be accomplished for the approximate amount allocated for the instrument. This recommendation might include the replacement of selected pads and corks on woodwind instruments and the cleaning and restringing of French horn valves as well as a host of other minor adjustments and repair services. Once the extent of this work has been agreed upon, it should be recorded in specific terms and verified when the instrument is returned from the shop.

Making Purchases—Spending the Budget

Once the approval of a budget request has been finalized, immediate steps should be taken to make the authorized purchases. Prompt action on the part of the director permits other school personnel involved in the purchasing process to do their work more efficiently. Delivery of major items of equipment and supplies as well as instrument-repair service can require 90 days or more. Prices of equipment not secured by bid can fluctuate upward. All of these factors encourage prompt action in making budget expenditures.

Standard Purchase-Request Procedure

Most school districts follow a formalized procedure for requesting a purchase even after the budget has been approved and the source of funding has been identified. Regardless of what particular forms and procedures are required, the band director should be prepared to supply specific and completely detailed information about (1) the name and description of the item to be purchased, and (2) the exact name, location, and complete address of the source where the item is available. Three sources are normally required for bid items.

A request for the purchase of a specific item of music or equipment would include a complete description. The following information is usually necessary and should be provided in sequence.

1. Quantity (amount, number of pieces, pairs, sets, etc.)
   Example: 12 each, 6 pair, 3 sets, 10 books, 1 arrangement, 1 repair, 1 overhaul
2. Item or Service
   Example: music lyres, drum sticks, pads, method books, march music, playing condition, alto saxophone
3. Description of the item (model number, style, serial number, publisher, arranger, composer, color, finish, etc.)
4. Additional requirements of supporting information (especially important on bid items)
   Example: complete with Bach 6½ AL mouthhpiece including lyre, deluxe case, and canvas zipper cover
   no alternate brand and model will be considered
5. Cost information (list price normally quoted)
6. Source of supply
   Example: Name of Business
   Street and mailing address
   City, State, Zip
   Telephone number

This information would then be incorporated in an actual request for the purchase and initiation of service for items appearing on the band budget. (See Figure 2-3.)

Band Department
Central High School
Date

Memorandum

TO: Business Manager
FROM: Director of Bands
RE: Request for Purchase

Purchase of the following items of equipment and service approved as a part of the Band Budget on June 12 is requested for delivery on or before August 15.

		Unit Cost	Total
12 ea.	MUSIC LYRES, Straight shaft, for trumpet or sax	$ 2.24	$ 26.88
10 books	BEGINNING METHOD: *Division of the Beat, Part I,* by Haines & McEntyre, Pub. by Southern Music, for following: 2 flute, 4 B^b clarinet, 4 cornet/trumpet	3.50	35.00
2 arr.	MARCH MUSIC, Full Band, *Garland Entree* by King, Pub. by Barnhouse	6.50	13.00
1 repair	BARITONE SAX, King, Model 1007, SN 12-00621, playing condition as per estimate	27.00	27.00
1 ohaul	SOUSAPHONE, King, Model 1250, SN 1008925, complete overhaul & relacquer as per quotation	512.00	512.00
	Order from: Tri-State Music Company Street Address City, State, Zip		

Figure 2-3   Request for purchase.

Bid Items:

2 each	BASS CLARINET, Buffet, Model R 26 1191, Key of B♭, w/single register vent. Complete with mpc, lyre, attached floor rest, and deluxe case.	$1128.00	$2256.00
1 each	FRENCH HORN, Conn, Model 8-D in F-B♭, Finish 60, complete with mpc, deluxe case, & canvas zipper cover	1050.00	1050.00

Submit invitation to bid with following information to dealers listed below:

School reserves the right to accept bid for any single item or to reject any and all bids. All bids must specify delivery date.

Band Instruments, Inc.
Street address
City, State, Zip
Telephone

Tri-State Music Co.
Street address
City, State, Zip
Telephone

National Band Supply
Street address
City, State, Zip
Telephone

Figure 2-3 (continued)

BIBLIOGRAPHY

Bollinger, Donald E. *Band Directors Complete Handbook* (West Nyack, NY: Parker Publishing Company, 1979)

Kinyon, John. *The Instrumental Music Director's Source Book.* (Sherman Oaks, CA: Alfred Publishing Co., 1982)

Otto, Richard A. *Effective Methods for Building the High School Band.* (West Nyack, NY: Parker Publishing Company, 1971)

Robinson, William C., and James A. Middleton. *The Complete Band Program.* (West Nyack, NY: Parker Publishing Company, 1975)

3

Starting Beginners
on Band Instruments

Before embarking on a rather detailed plan for starting a successful band program, it seems appropriate to say just a few words about the importance of this phase of band teaching. If is safe to say that most poor band programs in the secondary schools are the result of mismanagement of the beginning and junior high school phases of instruction. There is nothing more important to the overall success of a band program than beginning classes which are properly selected and correctly taught. Poor instruction within the first six weeks of a beginner's history can be the single most limiting factor in the student's playing career. Mistaught concepts of embouchure and breathing for the average student are extremely difficult to change in later years without the aid of private instruction. After such students reach high school age they seldom have the desire or patience for the kind of remedial effort which might make their playing productive.

With this brief admonition of caution and hopefully with a keen respect for the task at hand, here are some guidelines about what instruments to make available to beginning bandsmen and when to start them.

GRADE LEVEL AND LENGTH
OF INSTRUCTIONAL PERIOD

The trend for starting beginners in the early grades (i.e., 4th and 5th) has steadily moved upward. Many schools now start band instruments in the 6th or 7th grade. This has been encouraged by the concept of grouping grades 6, 7, and 8 in a "middle school," thereby separating grades 9 and 10 in a "mid high" school. It has long been my feeling that the late 6th grade or early 7th grade is the ideal time to approach beginning band instruction. The physical development of the student at this age permits much faster progress than in the 4th or 5th grade. Because of this accelerated progress, general interest and intensity will be more easily maintained. However, the one major factor to be taken into consideration is that the student must be available for at least one 40 minute period each day. If this is possible within the school schedule at the 6th grade level, we have (perhaps) an ideal teaching situation; if not, the beginning class would best be delayed until grade 7, assuming that the student could then be available on a daily basis.

Meeting students in either the 5th or 6th grade on an alternate-day schedule often increases the risk of "drop-out." This kind of a schedule is usually coupled with the disadvantage of a shorter period of 30 minutes or less. When such instruction takes place in separate grade schools where classes are small and instrumentation incomplete, it is easy for students to lose momentum and interest. The attraction they had for being a member of the "big band" is diminished, and taking "band" begins to seem more and more like "music lessons" in the worst connotation.

Using a beginning band class in the 6th grade which meets daily for 40 minutes as a model, the next step is to establish the correct instrumentation.

There is some flexibility in the different kinds of instruments to be included in beginning classes depending upon the time available later to make changes from basic to other instruments such as color clarinets and double reeds. The freedom to schedule large homogeneous classes of instruments will also have an important effect on the final decision.

RECOMMENDED INSTRUMENTS FOR BEGINNERS

Almost everyone agrees that the following instruments should be started: flute, B♭ clarinet, alto saxophone, cornet or trumpet, trombone, baritone, tuba, and percussion. From this point, filling out a complete instrumentation becomes a consideration of the availability of teaching time and the school-owned inventory of instruments. In most cases, the first five instruments listed are secured or owned by each student. The school is expected to own at least a skeletal inventory of all of the color woodwinds, tenor and baritone saxes, double reeds, French horns, baritones, tubas, and all percussion equipment except the basic snare drum.

A well-organized program which starts only the first seven winds plus percussion in the 6th grade would then plan on an orderly transition to a more complete instrumentation in the 7th grade, and would presume the 8th and 9th grade band to be a balanced independent ensemble. Under such circumstances, the changes might be made as follows:

Beginning Instrument	Change to
Flute	possibly oboe and bassoon
B♭ clarinet	alto or bass clarinet, contra-bass clarinet, oboe, and bassoon
Alto saxophone	tenor saxophone, baritone saxophone, bassoon, or oboe
Cornet/Trumpet	French horn (baritone or tuba)
Trombone	none
Baritone	none
Tuba	none
Percussion	expand to other percussion

Under less ideal circumstances and perhaps more realistically, the performing unit would be a combination of 7th and 8th grade students. Some of the changes after completion of grade 6 could then be done during the summer or with individual help outside of the regular instruction period.

CHANGING TO OTHER INSTRUMENTS

It is necessary to anticipate the problems of what to do with the instruments of students who are asked to change to another instrument. There are numerous ways to alleviate these problems, and the simplest solution would be to encourage all beginners on certain instruments, such as clarinet or cornet, to negotiate their horns on a rental agreement which many music merchants make available. By this means, a parent simply pays a fee considered to be rent on the instrument and is free to return it without further obligation when changing to another. Students who are in the process of buying their instruments have no reservations about learning to play another when furnished without cost by the school; they often prefer to keep their original instruments and continue playing them when the occasion permits. There are also many times when changing to another horn can be beneficial to the progress of the student. It is not uncommon that a cornet or trumpet player, unable to develop range, can make an acceptable French horn student. The B♭ clarinet student with "slow fingers" often feels more comfortable on one of the larger clarinets.

Keep in mind that under certain conditions a beginner may start on any instrument of the band. Small programs which have fewer numbers in the beginning classes make it possible for a skilled teacher to manage all of the instruments quite successfully.

BASIC ORGANIZATION AND RECRUITMENT

The entire process of organizing or recruiting beginning band classes may be divided into the following three steps:

1. *Orientation* through ensemble and individual instrument demonstration.
2. *Selection* of students through interest and aptitude testing.
3. *Finalization* of instrument choice or assignment in conference with the student and parent and enrollment in a band class.

There can be many variations in the manner in which these three basic steps are accomplished, depending upon the conditions existing in different school systems, but every successful program at some time will address the procedure whereby students are: (1) given the opportunity to explore the band and its separate instruments, (2) screened by test or other measure, and (3) assigned to or permitted to choose an instrument with the assurance that it will be provided and the child will be taught.

DEVELOPING STUDENT INTEREST
THROUGH ORIENTATION

"Who gets to play in the band?"
"How many students do you take into the band?"

"What are the names of all of the instruments?"

"Which is the easiest to play?"

"Which is the hardest?"

"Will it hurt my teeth?"

"How good do I have to be before I can start on an instrument?"

"What about my braces?"

These are just a few of the many questions in the mind of the student who is interested in learning to play a wind or a percussion instrument. Some kind of an orderly approach must be devised to organize that sea of inquiring minds that make up the potential beginner classes.

There are two ways to approach orientation sessions which will deliver the message about the band program to those who may be interested. Much, again, may depend upon how the particular school system is organized, and how the logistics of traveling from one school to another must be arranged.

The ideal manner in which to publicize the beginning band program and attract the attention of the students is to take a representative performing ensemble to the grade schools for a demonstration concert. If the emphasis is on starting 6th graders who are combined within a middle school, an 8th and 9th grade band from the same school could well be utilized. Large, smartly uniformed bands have the greatest impact but may also tend to be a bit impersonal and leave the students overawed. Still, a skillful demonstration of families of instruments in the band with emphasis on those instruments particularly needed will serve a useful purpose.

When confined to a classroom or an area too small to accommodate an entire ensemble, a group of representative instrumentalists in a performing ensemble will serve well. Some teachers prefer to use junior high students who formerly attended the same school for demonstration, feeling that rapport is more easily established with students close to the same age. On any such occasion it is always good to give special introductory recognition to any former student of the school, making a point of his or her success in the band to which others can relate.

Another approach to the orientation demonstration would be to transport all of the 6th grade students to the junior high school they will attend the following year. Here a demonstration ensemble can be set up to perform in its own environment for all of the visiting 6th graders. This approach has some advantages which will gain administrative support since it can serve a dual purpose. In addition to having these visitors hear the musical groups (which can include string and choral groups) and become acquainted with the band program, they can also be given a tour of the facilities, classrooms, and laboratories where they will continue their education. Brief talks about class scheduling and school policies can be included which will be of benefit to all students, even those who may not become members of the band in the future.

A third option which also has some advantages is to request permission to call on each grade school classroom with a small but representative group of advanced (junior or senior high school) students who will be used to demonstrate beginning instruments. The advantage of this method is that it permits closer personal contact with prospective students; most student also feel more comfortable to ask questions representing their true feelings and concerns about band instruction in their own classroom. The director has a much better chance to become acquainted on a first name basis and learn about especially talented students from the home room teacher. Perhaps the only disadvantage might be the large amount of time required to visit all of the classes in a large school system.

Regardless of which method of orientation is used, the following objectives must be accomplished:

1. Explain the simple steps for becoming a member of the beginning band class.
2. Impress upon the student that his parents or some adult needs to be a part of the planning in the decision to start band instruction.
3. Emphasize the enjoyment of learning to play an instrument and the fun of being a member of the band.
4. Isolate the various instruments of the band only to the extent that it will assist in explaining the student's role in making a choice. Some directors prefer to maintain complete control of choice, talking in terms of instrument "assignment."
5. Highlight the instruments of each family—woodwind, brass, and percussion—talking more about the instruments on which you want to start instruction and giving some indication of the number of beginners who may start on each instrument.
6. When using the full band for a demonstration, limit the performance; three numbers may be enough. Spend the rest of the time showing how the various instruments fit into the total picture.

7. Don't talk for long periods of time without letting the students hear sounds. Let them see where and how individual sounds are being produced.

8. When you are ready to close the presentation, be specific about the next step: "Next Thursday, boys and girls, I will visit Barton Elementary school. I'll bring with me a fun record of musical sounds (the test), and you will have a chance to show me how well you can listen. See you then!"

There are other considerations which will influence your approach to recruiting beginner classes. If you take over a band program that has been allowed to deteriorate to the extent of poor participation, you will want to attract larger numbers immediately. This objective can influence the kind of program the ensemble plays or the students you choose to highlight or use for demonstration. For example, an athletic hero or school beauty will certainly attract more attention, even if their musical skills are not particularly outstanding.

In a school which traditionally has had a very strong band program, the recruiting may be a self-sustaining process which does not require nearly as much effort in orientation and promotion. The standards of selectivity may be very high and you may prefer not to encourage participation as strongly since the interest will perpetuate itself.

SELECTION

Who should have the opportunity to learn to play an instrument? Should every child who is attracted by the flourish of the trumpet and gleam of polished brass be encouraged to start? Should only those whose parents can afford the cost be included? Is it fair to exclude those who appear to have little musical ability because the teacher knows they will never make a contribution to a performing ensemble? Is music not for everyone? Such questions probably need to be anticipated. Before the young band director has accumulated very many years in the profession, he or she will likely have the opportunity to address them.

We have all passed through an era when the watchword of our profession was "Every child for music and music for every child." In a sense, such a corollary is no more compelling than the statement:

"Every child for mathematics and mathematics for every child." Certainly, functional levels of mathematics for each child must be taught; the world around us demands that we count, make change at the drug store, and balance our bank statement. However, at some point our common sense tells us that a great majority of our children will have no practical need for more extensive training in the principles of mathematics.

And so it is with music. No one would question the wisdom of providing music training in the classroom from grades one through six. General music classes for junior high' and even in some senior high schools is certainly a necessary standard throughout the country. But at this point, specialized training in instruments of the band and orchestra or of the voice will be offered to those students who can predictably profit most, or whose desires can be supported by a high level of interest in music. In the area of band instruments, such a venture in new training must be matched in most cases by a substantial investment by the parents, and the role of the specialist now demands that he has the expertise to lend reasonable assurance that the investment is a wise one.

IDENTIFYING "MUSICAL TALENT"

The use of a test to measure the prospective student's "interest," "aptitude," or "talent" is a very common practice. It must be recognized that there is no valid measure of innate musical aptitude, but a number of good tests (even when mislabeled: "Talent Quiz") are available from music dealers and band instrument manufacturers. These serve not only to identify students with strong interest and the possibility of prior musical training, but also help to publicize the program and stimulate interest in other students.

One such test which has worked very well over a period of time is called the *Selmer Music Guidance Survey,* available from H&A Selmer, Inc. Elkhart, Indiana 46514. This survey is administered by means of a phonograph record or cassette tape, requiring written responses of a dual-choice nature on individual answer sheets. It is divided into four separate selections called (1) Pitch Recognition, (2) Chord Memory, (3) Melody Memory, and (4) Rhythm Memory. Actual administration requires about 20 minutes, but sufficient time must be allowed for the student to fill out additional information regarding home address and parents' names which are necessary in other stages of the recruiting plan. The survey requires a total of 60 responses from the student who may accumulate a maximum score of 120. Students in the 6th and 7th grade who score 95 or above will normally be quite successful in learning to play wind and percussion instruments. The individual sections of the survey have also been found to relate to areas of the students' strengths and weaknesses. For example, a student with a perfect score on rhythm memory is a good prospect for a percussion instrument; students with good melody memory and pitch recognition scores make good French horn and oboe students, a consideration especially important when placing students on school-owned instruments.

Administering the Survey.

Ideally the survey should be given by the band director in the students' home room. Giving the test there accomplishes two things: First, the home room limits the number of students being tested to a manageable size of 30 or less. The students, who tend to be a bit nervous about such a procedure, frequently develop a fear of "failing" and become apprehensive that they will not be permitted to enroll in a band class. Second, by going to the classroom in person, the band director has a first and important opportunity to represent the band program in a favorable light. Although use of the available time is critical, he can help the student to feel comfortable and relaxed, and begin to establish a rapport which will help to attract students.

Explaining the Music Survey

The presentation should begin with a brief summary of why the band director is in the classroom. Assure the class that the results of the survey will not be used to eliminate anyone from the opportunity to learn to play a band instrument. An opening statement might sound like this:

> *Central high school has long had a fine marching and concert band. They have represented our school, our town, and, in fact, all of us, very well in places like the Apple Blossom Festival in Washington, D.C., etc. The students in the Central High Band were once 6th graders in this same school. Some even sat behind your desks. These boys and girls enjoy playing in our band and staying together as friends as they go on through school. The reason we have a good band today is because they made a choice when they were your age to learn to play an instrument. Today I want to give you that same opportunity.*

Advise the students how and when the results of the procedure will become available. Usually a letter such as the one shown in Figure 3-1 is returned to all members of the class giving them not only their score, but other information about how to interpret the score and what the next step in the procedure may be. These letters can also be mailed directly to the parent at the home address provided on the test "information" section.

Be sure that each member of the class understand the preliminary examples given on the recorded version of the survey. Make a final check for broken pencil leads before proceeding. When the survey has been completed, answer any questions or review the next step in the procedure; then thank the home room teacher for her time and cooperation, and leave.

In large school systems containing many 6th grade classrooms, it is possible to enlist the aid of the classroom music teacher in administering the survey. This teacher is usually pleased to be included in the recruiting procedure and enjoys the opportunity to assess the musical skills of the students against the results of the survey. The disadvantage to the band director would be that of having one less personal contact with the students. Homeroom teachers, too, can often be of great additional help in providing more detailed information about students' work habits and skills through a simple assessment of student traits shown in Figure 3-2.

Grading the Survey and Reporting The Results

Scoring the surveys and returning the results in a letter should be done as soon as possible; a delay of more than a week will hurt the effectiveness of the campaign. This task is readily assisted by members of the high school band organization. Their involvement in the "beginner drive" makes them feel that they are an important part of the total music program. The same students (or their parents) can be of vital assistance in telephone work when preparing for the final important step of the recruiting operation.

Using the Results

The day before the first scheduled parents meeting, these student helpers can make brief telephone calls to the parents of students who indicate an interest in playing an instrument on their survey information cards. The callers must be instructed to be brief and pleasant in reminding the parents about the meeting without attempting to answer involved questions about costs or other details.

Student Name	School/Classroom	Score

Central Public Schools
Band Department
City, State
Date

Dear Parents:

Your child has recently taken a Music Guidance Survey to help evaluate his or her interest and potential for musical training on one of the band instruments. The results of this survey are shown at the top of this letter, the total score possible was 120. Those students who score 95 or better are especially encouraged to participate in band classes; however, any child who wants to study a musical instruments may do so.

All of the sixth grade students have had a chance to learn about the various instruments of the band through individual demonstrations. Many of the students already have a particular instrument in mind which they would like to play. To help them select an instrument which will best suit their particular physical characteristics, I will be at the school on *Tuesday* and *Thursday* evenings, *May 3 and 5*, beginning at 6:00 p.m. each evening. At that time the instruction program will be fully explained and each child will be individually interviewed.

Attached to this letter is additional information concerning the band program. It will be necessary for an adult to accompany any student who wants to enroll for band instruction. If for some reason it is not possible to attend either of the above meetings, feel free to call for a special appointment. (Telephone number)

Yours for Better Bands,

Director of Bands

Figure 3-1   Sample letter to parents.

Student's Name   School/Classroom   Score

(To be completed by the classroom teacher; information will be kept confidential.)

1. This student's grade average falls in the _____.
   _____ upper third of the class
   _____ middle third of the class
   _____ bottom third of the class

2. This student's standardized test scores indicate _____.
   _____ superior achievement and ability
   _____ above average achievement and ability
   _____ average achievement and ability
   _____ below average achievement and ability

3. This student is generally _____.
   _____ a good worker
   _____ an average worker
   _____ difficult to motivate

4. Basic instruction is communicated to this student _____.
   _____ easily
   _____ with some repetiton
   _____ with much repetition

5. This student _____.
   _____ is well behaved
   _____ usually abides by the rules
   _____ 's a discipline problem

6. Will this student have problems making passing grades in junior high school?
   _____ yes
   _____ no

7. This student _____.
   _____ has a strong competitive spirit
   _____ has an average competitive spirit
   _____ does not enjoy having to compete

8. Does this student work well with other students?
   _____ yes
   _____ no

Figure 3-2   Music Student Profile.

9 This student seems to be _____.
  _____ a follower
  _____ a leader
  _____ neither

10. Would this student's family have difficulty financing an instrument?
  _____ yes
  _____ no
  _____ possibly

Figure 3-2 *(continued)*

Special note should be made of students with unusually high scores. These students are sometimes candidates for school-owned instruments if the parents are unable to afford their own. The director may want to follow up on such students who do not appear with their parents at the regular meetings, since it is not uncommon for the parents of good potential students to miss such a meeting. A follow-up call the next day, however, can often produce good results.

CHOICE OR ASSIGNMENT OF INSTRUMENT

Some advanced preparation for the final step of the beginner campaign is important. If only one band director in the school system must approve the final choice of instrument for each beginner, the task can become most time-consuming. If a large number of students (30 to 60) enroll, at least two separate meetings will be required to properly manage all of the participants.

Organizing the Parents Meeting

It is always a good plan to address the group as a whole at the beginning of the meeting. A mature student, or a parent helper, should be stationed at the door to take names, addresses, and phone numbers of all who attend for future reference; some parents may have to leave before having an opportunity to discuss their choice in person. Hand each parent the information regarding the beginning band program (see Figure 3-3) which must be adjusted to fit your particular plan. This information will answer many traditional questions while they are waiting for the meeting to begin or while they are waiting to talk individually.

SOME ANSWERS about your band program.

1. Instruction is provided by school-employed teachers free of charge.
2. Band is scheduled one period each day as a part of the regular school curriculum.
3. Extra group help is often available before and after school without additional charge.
4. Paid private instruction is desirable after the first semester of class instruction; however it is not required.
5. Most beginners start on the following student-owned instruments: Flute, B♭ Clarinet, Alto Saxophone, Cornet/Trumpet, Baritone, Trombone, Tuba, and Percussion.
6. A few students with good academic records and high music test scores may transfer to school-owned instruments after the first semester or school term. These instruments include: Oboe, Bassoon, Alto and Bass Clarinet, French Horn, and Baritone Saxophone.
7. Your child does not have to buy a new instrument to take band instruction; good used instruments of the approved brands are acceptable; consult your director.
8. Certain manufacturer's instruments are preferred over others; this information will be provided.
9. All music dealers make new instruments available on some type of "trial" plan. This plan permits your child to use the instrument for one semester upon payment of the initial deposit. At the end of the trial period you may continue with regular installment payments or return the instrument without further obligation. Some dealers will also make the instrument available for regular monthly rental payments in which case there is no obligation to purchase the instrument.
10. Summer band classes will begin in August. This is a pre-school year program designed to give the beginners a head start. It will be most beneficial to start your child at that time.
11. Most band music is furnished by the school; each child will need to purchase a few additional materials at a nominal cost.
12. Band is a year-long activity available from the sixth through the twelfth grades. During junior high school most band students may also take part in athletic activities.
13. After you have completed arrangements for an instrument it will be delivered to the school so the director can personally instruct your child on proper assembly and care of the instrument.

Figure 3-3   Sample Description of a Band Program

Spend 15 minutes at the outset of the meeting explaining the band program, the need for instrumentation control in the classes, how to acquire an instrument, and the importance of parental support in matters of home practice and encouragement in general.

ACQUIRING AN INSTRUMENT

In many parts of the country, music dealers are invited to the school meeting to take part in this final step of the band beginner program, setting up shop and completing the financial agreement with the parent on the spot. This method is certainly the most convenient way for both parent and band director to finalize the assignment. However, in a community where there are multiple dealers or disagreement among the existing dealers as to who should have the privilege of selling instruments, it is best not to invite them to take part in this event. If this is the case you can only provide information to parents about the dealers and recommend that they make arrangements for a specific brand, model, or line of instrument. The final authority on inviting dealer participation must be your school principal or superintendent who will have definite feelings about the entire matter.

The Trial Rental Plan

All reputable music merchants make new instruments available to beginners on some kind of "trial rental" arrangement. Two of the most common plans are:

1. For a minimum down payment/deposit the child receives a new instrument of his or her choice to be used for a set period, usually 8 to 12 weeks. At the end of this period, the parents usually begin making regular installment payments toward the eventual ownership of the instrument, assuming that the child wants to continue study of the instrument.

2. For a minimum down payment/deposit the child again receives a new instrument, but regular monthly "rental" payments are required. There is no limit to the length of time the instrument may be rented under such an agreement. However, some dealers will actually give the instrument to the student at the end of a specified number of payments.

The important difference between these two kinds of "trial" arrangements is that the parent is not committed to make a decision about financial responsibility for full payment under the second arrangement, while the first agreement requires a decision at the end of the "trial" period. At that time the parent begins regular payments with interest on the note toward eventual ownership of the instrument. In reality, there is little difference between the actual cost of the instrument in either plan, but with the perpetual rental plan the parent is never committed to the purchase of the instrument.

A third variation of the trial rental plan is one in which all beginners start on a supply of either music dealer- or school-owned, used instruments. At the end of a specified period, usually a semester, the student must then buy a new or approved used instrument to continue in the program.

Regardless of which plan or variation is used, the first concern must be the well-being of the child and the band program. Keep in mind that some students will drop out of the program, and at that time will need to schedule another class activity. Since almost all school systems have limited flexibility for moving students from one class to another in the middle of a school term, a child who must complete the semester in a band class against his or her will can be a serious morale or discipline problem. A letter such as the example shown in Figure 3-4 should be used to inform parents of student progress and the teacher's recommendation at the close of some predetermined period of instruction.

IRVING PUBLIC SCHOOLS
Instrumental Music Department

Dear Band Parent:

Your child has been taking instrumental music training for a period of eight weeks, and I'm sure you would like some indication of the progress made.

One of the most important parts of doing good work in music is regular home practice. If your child has kept an accurate record of home practice in the back of the instruction book, you can tell how this has influenced his or her progress. Your encouragement in keeping the practice record is important.

The items checked below will help you to determine the progress made by your child.

Figure 3-4 Sample letter to parents.

ATTENDANCE: Absent from band class __ times.

HOME PRACTICE: _____ Does more than average.

_____ Does enough to keep up with the class.

_____ Should do more.

ATTENTIVENESS: _____ Always attentive in class.

_____ Usually attentive.

_____ Fails to pay attention frequently.

INTEREST: _____ Always alert and interested.

_____ Usually interested.

_____ Does not seem interested in class work.

ABILITY TO PLAY ASSIGNMENTS ALONE:

_____ Plays exceptionally well with good sound, rhythm, and pitch.

_____ Performs satisfactorily.

_____ Always makes an honest effort.

_____ Plays little if any.

RECOMMENDATION FOR FURTHER INSTRUCTION:

_____ Student has an excellent start and should continue to do well.

_____ Has a fair start but due to illness or other interruptions will need to work to catch up.

_____ Student seems to lack interest or ability to justify further training at this time.

If for any reason you would wish to discuss your child with me, please do not hesitate to call me at home (Phone Number) or at school (Phone Number).

Sincerely,

Band Director

Figure 3-4   *(continued)*

CONTROL OF CLASS INSTRUMENTATION

The band director must maintain control of beginner class instrumentation. The success of the total program is all based upon correct decisions made at this stage. Both parents and students must be made to realize the importance of controlled instrumentation.

They should be encouraged to formulate a second or even a third choice of instrument in case it becomes necessary to change. Here are some limiting factors which influence instrument choice:

1. General size and build of the student.
2. Size of the hands and fingertips; students with very thin fingertips cannot cover the tone holes of the clarinet.
3. Size of the mouth and structure of the lips; a large protruding "cupid's bow" makes playing the flute more difficult.
4. Very heavy mouth and lip structure is better suited to trombone, baritone, and tuba mouthpieces, rather than cornet, trumpet, or French horn.
5. Immediate plans for dental braces preclude starting on any brass instrument; saxophone, clarinet, or percussion will minimize such a problem.
6. Physical malfunction of the epiglottis or a cleft palate are complicating factors on wind instruments and must be diagnosed on an individual basis; if the student can sustain reasonable air pressure when blowing against a closed tube or container such as a Coke bottle, there is some hope; otherwise percussion or flute, which takes less air pressure, is a better choice.

It is a good idea to have several different kinds of mouthpieces available for illustration when making a point about specific recommendation.

A visual record of instrumentation progress can be maintained on the blackboard for all to observe as each assignment is finalized. Such a chart maintained by a student helper might look like Table 3-1 by the end of the first evening:

Table 3–1 INSTRUMENTATION FOR 40-PIECE BEGINNING BAND CLASS

Instrument:	Flute	Clar.	Sax.	Cor./Tpt.	Trom.	Bar.	Tuba	Perc.
Number of openings:	4	12	2	8	5	2	2	5
Openings filled:	‖	‖‖‖‖ ‖	‖	‖‖‖‖	‖	‖	‖	‖‖‖

Such a record helps parents and students alike fit their thinking into the need for limitation and regulation of the kinds of instruments which can enter classes.

CONCLUDING A SUCCESSFUL CAMPAIGN

In completing a beginner drive for band students there will always be several days spent contacting parents unable to schedule the meetings, or students who vacillate or change their minds. Again, the director will want to carefully screen his records for students who made high test scores or who expressed interest in band but did not make an effort to become a part of the program. A simple telephone call to the home often produces positive results and can bring a child into the music program who deserves the opportunity to learn to play an instrument.

As we prepare to move into the instructional phase of the beginner program we must be certain that music dealers, students, and parents alike understand that the beginner's first exposure to a new instrument must be done at school under the supervision of the band director. Unsupervised exploration of a new instrument in the hands of a child invariably produces bent keys, damaged valves, and a host of minor or major problems which impede the teaching process.

BIBLIOGRAPHY

Bulletin: Successful Recruiting. (Elkhart, IN: The Selmer Company, 1981)

Holz, Emil, and Roger E. Jacobi. *Teaching Band Instruments to Beginners.* (Englewood Cliffs, NJ: Prentice-Hall, 1966)

Hovey, Nilo W. *The Administration of School Instrumental Music.* (Melville, NY: Belwin-Mills Publishing Corporation, 1952)

Kuhn, Wolfgang. *Instrumental Music.* (Boston: Allyn & Bacon, 1965)

Maddy, Joseph Edgar. *Instrumental Technique for Orchestra and Band.* Florence, KY: Willis Music Company, 1945)

Pizer, Russell A. *Administering the Elementary Band.* (West Nyack, NY: Parker Publishing Company, 1971)

4

A Master Plan
to Develop
Performing Ensembles

The beginning band program originates under guidelines of controlled instrumentation which must logically be continued through an entire system of performing ensembles. This is called a "Master Plan" which will provide for balanced instrumentation in performing groups in junior high and high school. Without this kind of thoughtful planning and control there is no real pattern to the development of the various bands in a school system, and the possibility of assembling musically satisfying ensembles is left purely to chance.

COMMON FACTORS THAT INFLUENCE ENROLLMENT AND DROP OUT

Even when the instrumentation of beginner classes is carefully selected, there will be many changes as the group continues through their next six years in the school system. The three most common reasons for these changes are: (1) student drop-out, (2) student move-out, and (3) the change of school district attendance zones in an expanding community. The director has very little control over students who move out of the district or who are moved to another school by administrative edict. However, it would be worthwhile to examine some of the conditions which influence students who drop out of the band program at some stage before completing their senior year.

Problems During the Trial Period

The first period and set of circumstances which a student must hurdle is in the initial stages of learning to manipulate the mechanics of the instrument. This period would occur within the first three months, or the "trial period" of a child's musical training. If, during this time, the student has not learned what to do with his fingers, hands, and other physical equipment to produce a tone characteristic of the instrument, he or she is a good candidate for dropping out. The student is quite likely to become discouraged and will usually lack motivation for further progress. The four most common reasons for the development of problems at this stage in learning are:

1. The child lacks the musical and physical aptitudes necessary to progress at a rate equal to the average of his classmates.

2. The child has received poor instruction to the extent that he does not understand how to produce the results expected of him. This reason can also include instruction from a well-qualified teacher lacking in patience or understanding, or one too busy telling the student about how to play the instrument without letting him put it to his lips and try.

3. The child's time and energies are overdiversified; he has too much to do. In such cases, instrumental music training has usually been thrust upon the child by a parent who insists upon him taking piano, dancing, art, etc. There is not time in the daily schedule for successful progress in so many endeavors. Band is all too frequently the first to be eliminated because of the cost of the instrument.

4. Lack of encouragement by parents. Practice interferes with television or irritates the father or mother after a hard day's work. The instrument makes too much noise.

Problems with Continued Participation

The second general period when drop-outs occur is after successful completion of the first year, and the student must move on to another school campus, such as a middle school, junior high, or high school. The transfer from one location to another generally offers opportunities for participation in school activities of a broader scope. Furthermore, the prospect of changing band directors sometimes becomes a critical factor in the child's continuing interest in band. The student's interest can change to the exclusion of the band program for one of the following reasons:

1. The child's interest was falsely motivated at the outset. This student may have been the victim of an overenthusiastic parent who promoted band to prevent his participation in football. The child's only reason for starting band instruction may have been for identification with his peer group or the admiration of a television personality, rather than a genuine curiosity and desire for musical expression.

2. The child has failed to find the gratification dependent upon recognition of his efforts and accomplishments. The opportunities for ego reinforcement in class recitation and performance were never provided by the teacher.

3. The student lacks the energy, ambition, or time to achieve the level of his own, or peer group, standards. While those around him win medals, achieve first chair, and are chosen for All-District or All-State groups, this student lacks the drive and intensity to achieve these rewards himself. He begins to look around for other activities in which he can excel for recognition, and with less effort!

4. The student is subjected to pressure from outside sources such as athletic coaches, school patrons, relatives, girl or boy friends, etc. Inter-school recruiting for other activities such as the school yearbook, newspaper, speech and drama clubs, pep clubs and drill teams also take their toll.

Anticipating Student Attrition

Some of these reasons for dropping out are difficult to combat and students leaving the band program may well be making the best decision. The most important thing the band director can do is to make each day of band instruction an experience worthwhile and progressive toward a goal. The act of treating the student fairly in a democratic environment, and teaching him competently will be the most effective tool in holding him in the program.

Knowing that students will leave the program for various reasons may not make it any more palatable, but it does allow us to develop a realistic approach toward keeping the ensemble intact. Actual numbers of students who leave will vary greatly, depending upon the type of community which populates the school system. Schools built in traditional multiprofessional communities will probably be the most stable, and the rate of attrition in a band program which is well organized and supported will be less than others. Schools which grow up in conjunction with government or military activities will show a high rate of attrition as the parents of these students are transferred in and out of the community depending upon the government's need for such personnel.

Schools in heavy industrial areas will be as stable as that particular industry; variations in productivity and economic health will likely be reflected in school stability. Traditionally schools in rural and agricultural areas are quite stable, since the fortunes of the citizens are rooted in the land which does not move. Larger metropolitan school systems will show a much higher drop-out rate. These band programs often exist in a somewhat less personal atmosphere and students have more options to occupy their time. They live in diverse neighborhoods and place less value on the social aspects which develop in small-school band programs.

Table 4-1 shows some broad guidelines which may help in predicting the number of students who will at some time leave an organized band program. Predicting *who* these students may be and *what* instrument they play is, of course, not possible. It may be surprising or even disconcerting to recognize the fact that only about one-half of all students who start band instruction in the 6th grade will still be in the program at the time of their graduation from high school.

Tables 4-1 and 4-2 illustrate two periods when the percentage of drop-out is the highest: (1) the first year of instruction (taking into account those students who will withdraw from the class at the end of the trial period), and (2) that time when the student will have to change teachers, schools, or both. The drop-out rate between grades at other times is less.

If we follow the same beginner class of 40 students through their high school band career, the class might reflect a projection of attrition shown.

Table 4–1   PROJECTION OF ATTRITION (Grades 6–9)

Program Characteristic	Entering 6th Grade	Entering 7th Grade	Entering 8th Grade	Entering 9th Grade
Maximum Stability:	Bal: 40	- 6 (15%) Bal: 34	- 3 (10%) Bal: 31	- 3 (10%) Bal: 28
Average Stability:	Bal: 40	-10 (25%) Bal: 30	- 6 (20%) Bal: 24	- 5 (20%) Bal: 19
Mimimum Stability:	Bal: 40	-14 (35%) Bal: 26	- 8 (30%) Bal: 18	- 5 (30%) Bal: 13

(Loss per Year from 40 Member Beginner Class)

Table 4–2   PROJECTION OF ATTRITION (Grades 10–12)

Program Characteristic	Changing school to the 10th Grade	Entering 11th Grade	Entering 12th Grade
Maximum Stability:	- 4 (15%) Bal: 24	- 2 (10%) Bal: 22	- 2 (10%) Bal: 20
Average Stability:	- 5 (25%) Bal: 14	- 3 (20%) Bal: 11	- 2 (20%) Bal: 9
Minimum Stability:	- 5 (35%) Bal: 8	- 2 (30%) Bal: 6	- 2 (30%) Bal: 4

This simple exercise in studying the cumulative effect of dropout rates in the band program can serve two useful purposes:

1. The dramatic numbers of students who are lost under varying degrees of teaching and program effectiveness should be cause for sober reflection. The large numbers of students who leave our music programs each year will certainly serve to weaken the state of the art. A disenchanted dropout can easily grow up to be an influential school patron whose support of the band program will always be in question.

2. While these figures are to some extent hypothetical, students *do leave* the music program in a predictable manner. This must be accepted as a fact in the professional life of the band director and

managed with appropriate measures to maintain balanced instrumentation for the effective performance of music.

DEVELOPING THE MASTER PLAN

In making further use of the process of predicting numbers of students who will leave the band program, a more complete "Master Plan of Instrumentation" can be developed. The typical class of 40 beginners will be used for this purpose. Again, no effort need be expended on who or what instruments may drop out of the program, but rather what adjustments in instrumentation must be made as a result of declining numbers.

The master plan shown in Figure 4-1 is based on the drop-out rates set forth in the guidelines for a band program with maximum stability which exists under more ideal circumstances. Beginners are shown to start in the 6th grade, with the junior high performing ensemble in grades 8 and 9. Such a plan would make it possible to promote the beginners into a 7th grade "intermediate" class to continue their instruction. The high school band in such a plan would consist of students in grades 10, 11, and 12.

Although a more detailed discussion of band instrumentation will be covered later, some observations can be drawn from the progression of basic instrumentation to the more complete instrumentation shown on the plan.

One of the big advantages of the four-grade, "middle school-junior high" structure is that it permits an extra year of development in the 7th grade before switching some students to other instruments. The full instrumentation is developed within the 8th and 9th grades. Notice too, that the totals at the bottom of each grade level reflect the declining numbers due to natural attrition.

School-Owned Instruments

The inventory requirements of school-owned instruments will be a controlling factor in making changeovers when filling out the complete band. Rarely is it recommended that more than one student share an instrument; the notable exceptions might be the baritone and tuba which, because of their size, are not transported out of the building for home practice as often as the other instruments. A schedule of practice time within the band room area must be arranged for these students if they are expected to make the same kind of progress as the other students.

Conclusions

We can conclude from the examination of the Master Plan that:

1. Under somewhat ideal circumstances a class of 40 beginners started each year at the 6th grade level will adequately staff a junior

Instrument	Jr. Grades: 6	7	8	9	*Inventory Requirements	Hi Sch Grades 10	11	12	*Inventory Requirements
Flute.........	4	4	3	3		2	1	1	
Piccolo							1		1
Oboe........			1	1	2	1	1		2
Bassoon.......			1	1	2	1		1	2
Bᵇ Clarinet.....	12	10	5	5		4	4	3	
Eᵇ Sop									
Eᵇ Alto				1	1		1	1	2
Bᵇ Bass......			1	1	2	1	1		2
Contra Bass..			1		1	1			1
Alto Sax.. ...	2	2	1	1		1	1	2	
Tenor Sax ...				1	1	1		1	2
Bari Sax. ...			1		1		1		1
Cornet/Tpt	8	6	4	4		3	3	3	
Fr Horn			2	2	4	1	2	2	4
Trombone	5	4	4	3		3	2	2	
Baritone	2	2	2	1	7	1	1	1	3
Tuba..........	2	2	1	1	6	1	1	1	3
Percussion.....	5	4	4	3	full percussion	2	2	2	full percussion
Snare		(1)	(1)	(1)		(1)	(1)	(1)	
Bass/cym		(1)	(1)	(1)		(1)	(1)		
Tympani.....		(1)	(1)					(1)	
Keyboard....		(1)	(1)	(1)			(1)		
TOTALS	40	34	31	28		23	22	20	

*Instruments which are normally owned by the school system.

Figure 4-1 Master instrumentation plan.

high school 8th and 9th grade performing ensemble of 59 players. This will ultimately develop into a high school band in grades 10, 11, and 12, of 63 players. Both provide adequately for excellent balance and the possibility of rewarding musical results. Those directors who are motivated to foster larger groups or more than one band in high school will have to seek out circumstances which permit the opportunity to start more beginners.

2. The importance of correctly selected and taught beginner band classes looms ever more significant; the need for flexibility in changing instruments to accommodate proper band balance magnifies the responsibility for sound teaching within basic families of instruments. We can see the importance of a larger number of beginners on clarinet and cornet/trumpet because they represent the two basic areas of reed and valve instruments so critical to complete band instrumentation.

BIBLIOGRAPHY

Colwell, Richard. *The Teaching of Instrumental Music.* (New York: Appleton-Century-Crofts, 1969)

Jones, Archie N. *Music Education in Action.* (Dubuque, IA: William C. Brown, 1964)

Norman, Theodore Frederick. *Instrumental Music in the Public Schools.* (Philadelphia: Oliver Ditson Company, 1941)

5

How to Select and Use Teaching Materials

The study of a beginners method book or series should be done with care. There are many good method books available, and any one of them can be successfully used if the teacher fully understands the limitations of the material as it is presented. The decision about which particular method book to use may already have been made if a certain book has been adopted in a school prior to the director's arrival. However, the occasion will arise when the choice must be reviewed and the following information will be of help in an intelligent evaluation of any book or series. Even when a choice of methods is not involved, a thorough study of the book currently in use will be extremely helpful.

LIMITS OF BEGINNING METHODS

No method in existence is "complete" in the sense that it contains all the information needed to correctly instruct beginning instrumentalists. The authors of every book have to make concessions about what information to include and to assume that the teacher can supply the rest. (The teacher will find that some publications supply more complete information and will be more helpful in the first few years of teaching beginners.) Other series simply provide a "Conductor" book with a two staff score, leaving a great deal to the background and imagination of the teacher. As a teacher gains experience and knowledge in beginning techniques, a more individualized routine in the presentation of information will be developed. Such a teacher becomes less dependent upon information printed in the manual and even begins to supplement the student books with individualized material to strengthen and reinforce the text.

HOW TO STUDY A METHOD OR A SERIES

The following outline provides for an indepth study of any method or series. It will also serve to better prepare the teacher for the important role confronting him or her at the beginning of each semester or school term.

Construction and Makeup

1. Size of the book, material, print, quality, color, etc.
2. Illustrations.
   a. The instrument with parts clearly labeled
   b. The student, showing correct posture and hand and finger position (Should be appropriate age with current hair style, dress, or uniform)
   c. Fingering chart, readable and readily accessible, including trill chart when applicable
   d. Table of notes and note values
   e. Clear and uncluttered layout which emphasizes important points
3. Individual books should be available for each instrument, or material should appear in the appropriate register if used for more than one instrument.
4. Some series have a selection of coordinated material available for full band, solo, ensemble, and theory and technical development.
5. Note availability and dependence of prerecorded tapes to be used in conjunction with the book.

6. Preface should designate type of instruction for which book is designed: class, individual, homogeneous, or heterogeneous groupings.

General Information

1. Index.
2. Glossary of musical terms.
3. Authors, editors, instrumental consultants, and special contributors.
4. Background or history of the instrument.
5. Breathing, breath control, breath support.
6. Explanation of embouchure, tone production, articulation; presented in orderly steps for teacher's information.
7. Assembly and care of the instrument.
8. Mechanics of tuning the instrument.
9. System of numbering and reference to student pages.

Teaching Material

1. Clear explanation of the first steps in tone production on mouthpiece or headjoint alone.
2. First tones on the assembled instrument must be in a playable register and with enough fingers involved to control the instrument.
3. Explanation and illustration of staff, clefs, bar lines, and basic note values.
4. A logical system of rhythm sequence and introduction of patterns supported by melodies and exercises. Rhythms should be repeated in a variety of forms to avoid monotony but still provide continued drill. A common system of counting must be included to develop a rhythmic vocabulary.
5. Clarity in making the point upon first introduction of a new note, rhythm, or fundamental.
6. A balance of familiar tunes to hold the student's interest as well as technical studies and études characteristic of the instrument in the proper register.
7. Grouping of voices with both familiar and contrasting problems for drill purposes.

8. Balance of unison and harmonized material in which all may share in playing melody as well as parts characteristic of the instrument.

9. Book progresses at a constant and regular pace without hurrying across fundamental problems.

10. Periodic reviews of material covered in each major section; occasional written tests when appropriate.

11. Separate section providing all scales in keys covered in the book with arpeggios and articulated patterns.

12. Effective presentation of dynamics and phrasing with consistent use of breath marks and explanation of breath support.

13. The first book (or Part I) usually covers keys of C, F, B♭, E♭, and A♭, and time signatures in 4/4, 3/4, and 2/4. Second book (or Part II) includes one and two sharps, five and six flats, and cut time, 6/8 time, and 3/8 time.

Most items in the outline of evaluation are self-explanatory. Occasionally the teacher will not have sufficient experience to render a judgment about the relative worth of a particular area. In such cases, a comparison of two or more books will usually identify strengths and weaknesses within the area. A suggested form using this outline for the analysis of a beginner method appears in Figure 5-1.

Information Frequently Neglected

Some typical areas in which the teacher must be the source of more authoritative information are:

1. Correct formation of the playing embouchure. Most books and manuals provide only general information about lip tension, firmness of muscles, and some simple "do's" and "don'ts." The teacher must be able to describe and demonstrate the embouchure and produce an acceptable characteristic tone on every instrument.

2. Breathing, breath control, and breath support. The teacher must be able to demonstrate correct breathing and identify faulty techniques in the student. He must accurately describe specific muscular action in taking and holding air in the lungs in a manner which provides correctly-supported sound.

Name of Book or
Series   Publisher   Volume of Total

Author(s) and   Consultants

Additional Coordinated Books

Tape Recordings?

Score & Size: _____   _____   _____   _____
         Full   4/5 line   Piano/Cond   Type of
                                                    Binding

Student Books Published, First Tones, and Playing Range:

_____ Flute, ____ ;   ____to ____.   _____ Oboe ____ ;   ____to ____.
_____ E♭ Clar ____ ;   ____to ____.   _____ Bassoon _ ;   ____to ____.
_____ B♭ Clar ____ ;   ____to ____.   _____ Cornet/Tpt

                                                             _____ ;   ____to ____.
_____ E♭ Alto Cl_ ;   ____to ____.   _____ Horn in E♭/
                                                         B♭ _____ ;   ____to ____.
_____ Bass Clar _ ;   ____to ____.   _____ Horn in F_ ;   ____to ____.
_____ Alto Sax _ ;   ____to ____.   _____ Trombone
                                                         _____ ;   ____to ____.
_____ Tenor Sax
            _____ ;   ____to ____.   _____ Baritone, TC
                                                         _____ ;   ____to ____.
_____ Bari Sax _ ;   ____to ____.   _____ Baritone,
                                                         B.C. _____ ;   ____to ____.
                                                         Tuba _____ ;   ____to ____.

Percussion:

_____

_____ Snare; Rudiments: _____   _____   _____   _____   _____
___ B.D./Cym ___ Traps ___ Mallets ___ Bells ___ Marimba ___ Xylophone
___ Tympani; Other: _____

Time Signatures: ____ on page ___; ___ on page ___; ___ on page ___;
                      ___ on page ___; ___ on page ___; ___ on page ___;

Figure 5-1   Beginner and intermediate text analysis.

Key Signatures: ____ on page ____; ____ on page ____; ____ on page ____;
____ on page ____; ____ on page ____; ____ on page ____;

Note Values: ____ on page ____; ____ on page ____; ____ on page ____;
____ on page ____; ____ on page ____; ____ on page ____;

Rhythmic Difficulty: __(example)__ on page ____; _____ on page ____;

_____ on page ____; _____ on page ____;

Articulation: Normal on page ____; staccato on page ____; legato on page
____; Trombone legato on page ____; Slur on page ____; accent on page
____;

Number of studies in: Unison ____; Duet ____; Three part or more
____;

Traditional tunes, e.g.: _____ _____

Etudes and studies,
e.g.: _____ _____

System of rhythmic counting: _____

Figure 5-1 *(continued)*

3. Beginning tone production. The common practice of getting a fundamental tone or buzz on the mouthpiece or headjoint of the instrument is seldom emphasized or illustrated in beginning books. Frequent reference to, or provision for, exercises of this kind are not included. They must be originated by the teacher, or the material in the book must be adapted to this important use.

4. Use of the tongue in starting the tone and in various styles of articulation. The minute detail in the correct use of the tongue in starting each tone and in learning legato tonguing, especially for trombone, is seldom available in the books. The teacher must draw from personal experience and be able to demonstrate and describe the subtle differences employed in the various woodwind and brass instruments.

5. Mechanics of tuning the instrument and the importance of playing in tune. This subject is not normally addressed in the beginning stages of teaching. At first, all instruments should be fully assembled with all mouthpieces, tuning slides, and other adjustable parts in the same relative position. However,

before the end of a full semester, the subject of matching pitches and tuning must be approached, and the art of learning to listen and adjust tones must begin to develop.

6. Presentation and regular practice in a system of counting rhythms. A number of books touch on this point. Some utilize the traditional syllables of "one-and, two-ee-and-uh" while others introduce word association such as "Miss-i-ssip-pi" for four sixteenth notes. The introduction and regular use of a system of verbalizing rhythms is critical to the full development of the potential musician. A suggested method of rhythm counting will be detailed next in this chapter.

7. Basic reference to phrasing and dynamics. Many teachers prefer to concentrate on the production of a full sound without requiring dynamic changes which might disturb the formation and control of the embouchure. However, since phrasing at this point relates to proper breathing, it seems appropriate that some system of breath marks be used to keep breathing uniform within the group.

COUNTING RHYTHM

The particular method of counting rhythms presented here may not necessarily be original but it has evolved over a period of time and provides a stable reference for vocal intonation of rhythmic problems.

Rhythmic Verbalization Related to Performance

The director who will take the time and trouble to teach this system along with the introduction of note values and refer to them on a regular daily basis will find that the student develops a confident understanding of rhythm in performance. Development of this system or any other provides an immediate frame of reference to any rhythmic problem which may arise in the rehearsal or classroom. Conversely, the lack of a system leaves both the conductor and the student without any common language for demonstrating and correcting the problem.

This particular system is based on the similarity and relationship of vocally intoning a note value and then actually playing it on the instrument. The use of traditional numbers and syllables is recommended, and the all-important subdivision of the beat is a constant factor to be defined with a down-up motion of the free hand while not playing.

When introducing the whole note, it should be intoned throughout the four-count duration on the beginning syllable of the first number while the free hand pats out the four counts with down-and-up motions on the knee. (See Figure 5-2.)

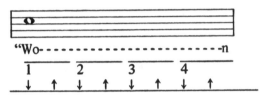

Figure 5-2

The following observations may be made:

1. By starting the syllable with "One" and sustaining the first sound through the four-count value of the note, the student approximates the use of the breath as he would in playing and sustaining the note.

2. While sustaining the value of the whole note, the student must remember the correct sequence and number of counts in the note, even though the actual definition of the separate beats and upbeats is being done by the hand on the knee. This action bears a similarity to keeping track of the beats mentally while playing the note on the instrument.

3. Instead of simply counting to four for the total value of the whole note, the student intones only the number on which the note originates for four counts, thus differentiating between four quarter notes which would also be identified by intoning each of the four counts. The pronunciation of the syllable corresponds to articulation on the instrument.

4. The source of the beat when first learning to count will be from the hand, not the foot. When the student puts the instrument in playing position utilizing both hands, the beat source must become a mental response which is the ultimate goal. This prevents dependence on the use of the foot in keeping the beat.

The system would then apply to other note values in the **manner** shown in Figure 5-3.

Complexity of rhythms can be expanded to keep up with student progress. Vocal intonation of the syllables continues to approximate articulation on the instrument.(See Figure 5-4.)

"Wo- - - - - - - -n Three- -Fou- - -r Wo- - -n Too- - - - - - - - - - - -oo

Figure 5-3

1- - - - - -2- -&- -3- - - - - - - - - - 1- - &- - 2- - &- - - - - - -4-e -&-u- -

Figure 5-4

Slow and fast 6/8 time can be added by using numbers on **each** beat of slow 6/8, and the word "trip-o-let" in combination with numbers in fast 6/8 time. (See Figure 5-5 and Figure 5-6.)

Rests may be treated silently or by verbalizing the word "rest" for the proper duration. Arrows locating the beats may be placed above the note to encourage perception of a larger area in reading music. (See Figure 5-7.)

Largo

1 2 3 4 - 6   1 - 3 - 5 -   1 2 - 4 ———

Figure 5-5

March

1 o let 2 o let   1 — let 2 o —   1 o — 2 - -

Figure 5-6

Figure 5-7

PRIMARY GOALS FOR BEGINNERS

Throughout the evaluation and analysis of beginning method books, the specific objectives of this phase of teaching must be clear. This will include (1) development of tone quality characteristic of the instrument, (2) ability to tongue in three basic styles: normally separated, staccato, and legato; and (3) an understanding of pulse and rhythm. These are fundamental mechanical skills which are the foundation of all musical performance. They are absolutely critical to the success of any and every band program and are most appropriately taught at the beginning level. As we will see later, these skills become the foundation in the art of making music. Other skills will, of course, be a part of early training but none are as critical as these. If for any reason, these skills become neglected or the student fails to master them, that student is doomed to a career of remedial learning or mediocre performance.

Continued Emphasis on Beginner Objectives

The first year of instruction must include a constant evaluation of student progress. The extent to which any method will contribute to the mastery of these fundamentals is a relative matter. As stated before, there is no "complete" book which will insure the achievement of these important goals. It is, however, the responsibility of the teacher to relate whatever material is used to the continuous assessment and evaluation of tone quality, articulation, and correct rhythmic placement of each sound in the measure. Figure 5-8 lists several resources you can use for beginning band methods.

During the teaching process it becomes easy to fall prey to acceptance of "average" or mediocre levels of achievement. Sometimes

Publisher	Title	Author(s)	Parts	Publication Date
Alfred	*Alfred's Basic Band Method*	Sandy Feldstein John O'Reilly	two	1978
Correlated Material:	Solo and Ensemble Book Theory Concèpts Book Cassette Practice Tape Individual Band Arrangements			
Belwin-Mills	*Easy Steps to the Band*	Maurice D. Taylor	one	1942
Belwin-Mills	*Belwin Band Builder*	Wayne Douglas	three	1957
Belwin-Mills	*First Division Band Method*	Fred Weber	four	1962
Correlated Material:	*First Division Melody Inst. Method*	Fred Weber		
	Fun With Fundamentals	Laas-Weber		
	Away We Go	Erickson, Ployhar, Weber		
	Solos for Each Instrument			
	Ensembles for Everyone	Acton Ostling		
	Concert Band Arrangements	Erickson, Ployhar, Osterling		
Belwin-Mills	*Band Today*	James D. Ployhar	three	1977
Correlated Material:	*Technic Today*	Ployhar		
	Concert Tody	Erickson, Osterling, Ployhar		
	3 Solos for each Instrument			
	Concert Band Selections	Erickson, Osterling, Ployhar		
	Notes For Today	George Zepp		
	Band-Sembles	Frank Erickson		
Hal Leonard	*Hal Leonard Elementary Band Method*	Harold W. Rusch	one two	1966 1961
	Hal Leonard Intermediate Band Method	Harold W. Rusch		1963 1974
	Hal Leonard Advanced Method	Harold W. Rusch		
	Learning Unlimited	Art C. Jenson		
Heritage Press	*Sessions in Sound*	Barbara Buehlman Ken Whitcomb	three	
Correlated Material:	*Pencil Sessions.*			
Kjoz West	*Best in Class*	Bruce Pearson	two	1982
Southern	*Division of Beat*	Harry H. Hains J. R. McEntyre	two	1980

Figure 5-8   Selected beginning band methods.

a given class or section of beginners seems to produce no one who is able to play with truly good quality, or a model to which the rest of the class aspire. This may make it necessary for the teacher to become more active in playing with the class as they drill on tone studies. Simple daily routines of the teacher playing a sound followed by individual student or class performance in sequence can provide a subtle stimulus. Continued diagnosis of the problem will provide the basis for daily (but often brief) reference to embouchure correction or better breathing and support. The important point is not how long it takes or how often it must be repeated, but rather that it *must* be done.

BIBLIOGRAPHY

Green, Eddie. *How to Get the Most Out of Method Books*. (Elkhart, IN: The Selmer Company, 1981)

Holz, Emil, and Roger E. Jacobi. *Teaching Band Instruments to Beginners*. (Englewood Cliffs, NJ: Prentice-Hall, 1966)

Kohut, Daniel L. *Instrumental Music Pedagogy: Teaching Techniques for School Band Directors*. (Englewood Cliffs, NJ: Prentice-Hall, 1973)

Neidig, Kenneth L. *The Band Director's Guide*. (Englewood Cliffs, NJ: Prentice-Hall, 1964)

6

Setting the Stage for Learning

There is a remarkable relationship between goals, achievement, and discipline. The influence or modification of behavior called "learning" is caught up within this trio of words describing that all-important element of effective teaching, and the relationship between the achievement of goals and discipline is one that must be made clear. The establishment of effective discipline mandates the identification of a worthwhile goal in music and identifiable progress toward that goal.

DISCIPLINE IN MUSIC

Discipline is a structural framework; a border or fence which channels appropriate acts in correct sequence toward a predetermined goal or conclusion. The achievement of a goal is sometimes as simple as prescribed repetition in learning to play a scale, and sometimes much more complex, like reshaping a feeling or an attitude which endangers mental health. Most goals can be attained with the correct exercises and energies. The prescription for attainment of the goal can usually be identified; only the discipline for achievement can serve to activate the modification of behavior.

The Importance of Planning

Learning best takes place within a controlled atmosphere of specific conditions. Although some kinds of learning, such as learning by experience or negative learning, can occur without actual control of the learning environment, lack of a controlled atmosphere leaves things to happen by chance, rather than by design. The band director who proceeds with a private lesson, a beginner class, or an ensemble rehearsal without a plan and some concept of an objective is, therefore, playing a game of chance. The odds for success under such circumstances is strictly a gamble, much as if a coin representing an investment is thrown into a slot machine while the owner stands waiting for the results. The number of people in our profession who "fly by the seat of their pants" is unacceptably high. These are the ones who ridicule the idea of a lesson (or any) plan, who feel that they can learn the score as the band reads a new piece of music, and who are comfortable with mediocrity.

The dimension of a successful band program includes a specific set of objectives to be achieved by a carefully planned procedure of recruiting beginners and instrumentating the ensemble. To effect the change in behavior and the development of skills in learning music, the stage must be properly set. Fortunately for the band director, many of the problems of the classroom teacher in modifying behavior do not exist in the band room. The study of instrumental music is not normally required of all students; those who come to study usually choose to do so.

Additionally, the screening process of selectivity has further insured the presence of students who have a high degree of interest in musical achievement. At least at the beginning, we are assured of almost complete agreement of the stated objective—to learn to play an instrument. Whether or not the student remains in agreement with this objective depends almost entirely upon the skill of the teacher.

Establishing the Need for Discipline

The productive examination of discipline must first determine its need and contribution to the band program. If there are no clearly stated objectives that both student and teacher understand, there is no real need for discipline. Discipline must be a fundamental precept for getting things accomplished. If no real plan for the achievement of objectives exists in the mind of the director, and has never been communicated or even dramatized to the student, a need for discipline is of little real concern. (Undisciplined acts that disturb the classroom will certainly inconvenience and irritate the teacher, but this kind of misbehavior hardly interrupts the plan for learning since one has never been formulated.)

In searching out a model of discipline in music education, be aware that there are some ways that discipline is *not* achieved. The act of striking a student with a stick of wood, the hand, or some other object does not produce discipline, nor is it characteristic of good discipline. Loss of control can momentarily reduce frustration in the teacher, but it produces anger, resentment, and fear in the recipient, and normally destroys the setting for learning. A teacher who commonly employs corporal punishment misunderstands the learning process and implies a lack of skill as a teacher.

Discipline is not embodied in the constant act of raising the voice in a threatening invocation. Students generally respond in an equally negative manner, or learn to accept it as commonplace, not worthy of response. Discipline in a classroom is also not so autocratic and dictatorial that every move is programmed in fear of other forms of reprisal.

The Final Objective: Self-Discipline

Real discipline is designed to promote learning. Real discipline originates in the director who has matured to a stage of leadership. Real discipline reacts positively to the possibility of both reward and punishment, and it is constantly striving to set the student free to become *self-disciplined*. Discipline functions within a framework of democratic principles which says that all men (including students and teachers) are created equal, but must also make, and observe, laws and rules. They must accept punishment if these rules are broken. Real discipline is an ideal vehicle for the language of the art of music which cannot speak its freedom until discipline is achieved. The close emotional interaction with the production of music makes discipline a natural ally to the goal of self-esteem which often becomes very difficult to separate from the satisfaction of the music performance.

GOALS AND DISCIPLINE IN THE CLASSROOM

What are the goals in the beginning band classroom, in the junior high and high school performing ensembles? Has the real purpose and intent of each teaching or conducting act been addressed? Assuming that the director/teacher has formulated these goals, have they been verbalized, explained, or in some other way communicated to the student? Have the rules or the structural framework been established by which these goals can be achieved? The fun in music, the reward, is in the making of music by learning to play the instrument. The achievement of such a goal requires certain appropriate acts in correct sequence. The implementation of this sequence is only achieved through discipline, imposed externally at first but eventually resolved and accepted within the student as self-discipline in order to be completely successful.

Practical Goals for Beginners

The following set of objectives might be a typical example for a twelve-week teaching period of beginning band students:

1. Arrival at a specific location at a correct time with all appropriate material and equipment.
2. An understanding of the exact behavior expected in this location during the period of time in which the class meets.
3. The ability to correctly assemble and care for the instruments and related equipment.
4. The ability to describe the embouchure or stick position and the basic muscular action by which the embouchure may be achieved.
5. The ability to describe the use and control of the breath, as well as accompanying muscular action.
6. Production of a tone and a quality which is characteristic of the instrument through formation of the correct embouchure and use of the breath.
7. Correct use of the tongue or the hand in starting the sound.
8. Correct posture and placement of the hands and fingers in producing specified tones or notes.
9. An understanding of certain fundamental terms relating to music and the instrument; identifying notes and rests visually and producing them correctly in duration and pitch.

10. Appreciation for the need and effect of outside preparation in practice.

Routine Objectives

Virtually all of these objectives must be achieved by instruction, demonstration, and imitation, used in combination or alone. It is often at this fundamental level that the need for discipline and an understanding of how it is accomplished is lost or never established.

The art of instruction requires the establishment of certain rules. For the objectives listed, these rules should be simply stated procedures for entering and leaving the classroom, how the scheduled time available during the period will be used, when and how the instrument is taken from the case, and all the other details of a fundamental organizational nature. These rules must be routinely reenforced as needed before any loss of classroom control might occur. Much of this type of instruction would parallel that which might take place in any other classroom of the school, but the reasons for responding to such a set of rules must relate to the overall goal of learning to play an instrument.

The next level of instruction is for the skill of achieving sound on a musical instrument. This involves demonstration and imitation, in addition to verbalized instruction. These procedures are not common to any other classroom activity and take place in a different environment of learning. The initial experiments in producing sound can easily degenerate to undisciplined noise, and a teacher must know when to rescue students from such a nonproductive activity or prevent it from happening in the first place. Such matters must be controlled by predetermined guidelines as students learn to respond to the first conducting gestures by the teacher. These conducting gestures are the sign language giving music students a first experience in group participation with the control of starting and stopping firmly in the hands of the director. Part of the fun and joy of music is when a class realizes the satisfaction of group response to a downbeat and the release which ceases the activity.

RECOGNIZING SOCIAL PROBLEMS

At the beginner level of instruction, discipline problems which may interrupt objective achievement are often social, or more appropriately, antisocial. Students at this stage continue to be self-motivated to some extent and maintain a desire to please. Even when dictatorial techniques of control are applied, students of beginner age will not rebel. This response unfortunately encourages the young teacher to continue the use of this method of repressive control, mistaking it for acceptable discipline. The teacher must know the difference between being firm and being rude. Students entering and leaving a classroom have access to moments of their greatest freedom and physical activity. The teacher's presence and influence is critical, even after correct patterns of band-room behavior are established.

The seating arrangement and physical setup is best prepared in advance although this may not always be possible when groups follow each other in the same facility with only a few minutes between classes. Still, the effect of prearranged seating is a stabilizing factor and well worth the extra trouble it may require. Even more important is seating which provides for avenues of easy access to each student during the early stages of instruction. Many teachers prefer that students be seated in simple long rows of chairs (see Figure 6-1) for maximum visual contact of both the student and the instrument. When the size of a beginning group makes such an arrangement impractical, the traditional semicircular arrangement by sections (see Figure 6-2) is still satisfactory but should leave room for at least two aisles for passage from the front or podium area to the last row in the room. Individual contact is extremely important in the beginning.

During the first semester of instruction, the placement of instruments in a concert arrangement is not as important as accessibility to the student. In a heterogeneous group, for example, it may be more important to have trombones and French horns in the front row so that their progress and problems can be more closely monitored. Each student should be provided with ample room for the instrument case or a place to rest the instrument when instruction is focused on use of the mouthpiece or head joint alone. When floor space permits, there are several advantages in having beginners bring their cases to where they are seated. Accessories normally kept in the case are readily available. At the close of the class period the teacher can continue to supervise the restoration of the instrument to its case as well as traffic patterns out of the room. This is not possible when all cases are kept in an instrument storage room which is isolated from the main rehearsal area. Dismissing young instrumentalists to put their horns in the instrument room often results in damaged equipment and discipline problems.

A natural tendency for students to cluster near each other as well as close to the teacher frequently inhibits effective instruction.

Students in close proximity find it more convenient to talk and create disturbances. The teacher who immobilizes himself behind a podium on a conducting stool tends to lose control over activity in the back two-thirds of the room. For this reason it is helpful to remain standing and move freely about the entire room at times during the instructional period.

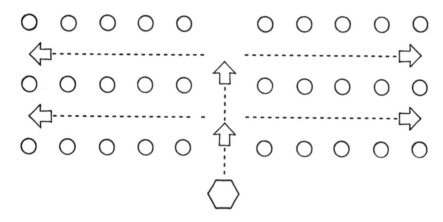

Figure 6-1   Straight-row arrangement in beginner seating.

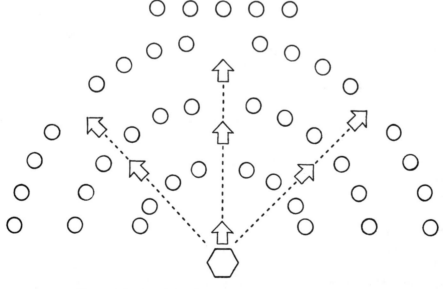

Figure 6-2   Traditional arrangement in beginner seating.

PROBLEMS CAUSED BY THE TEACHER

The social problems of discipline which may surface in beginning students usually result from individual conflicts which may originate outside of band class. These matters are best resolved by calm restraint or moving the students apart. The more serious discipline problems are nearly always originated by the teacher. Some of the more common teacher-induced problems are:

1. Failure to outline rules and procedures for classroom control
2. Absence from the classroom at critical times
3. Failure to give clear instructions or to speak with clarity
4. Lack of preparation for daily teaching objectives
5. Failure to address minor behavior problems and subsequent overreaction to their recurrence
6. Differing levels of reaction to similar behavior problems created by different students
7. Failure to begin class promptly
8. Failure to dismiss the class in time for the student to take proper care of his instrument and equipment without being late to the next class
9. Inconsistent or insecure instruction
10. Inconsistent reaction to playing errors; negative reaction to the same problem which drew no reaction the day before
11. Lecturing at length while horns grow cold and reeds dry out (Once actual playing starts, the teacher stops the group almost immediately to lecture further and the problem perpetuates itself.)

POSITIVE REENFORCEMENT AND MOTIVATION

Good discipline and good morale are closely related; both factors contribute to high achievements resulting in groups that are motivated. While students are sometimes self-motivated at this early age, the teacher must assume responsibility for motivation and inspiration in general. Some teachers have a personality and an approach to their work which is in itself motivational. The best example of such a characteristic is enthusiasm. Students find such an attitude contagious. However, the majority of band directors and teachers must work to develop such an enthusiasm throughout their professional life. Effective teachers devise or develop certain conditions within their bands and band classes which serve as a motivational catalyst.

In the early history of the band movement, it was common knowledge that some of the great conductors achieved results by ridicule, sarcasm, and open embarrassment of their playing personnel. This practice is not entirely absent from the public schools today. However, bands which achieve a successful reputation are more often the results of teaching which is based on positive reenforcement of student attitudes and skills.

Positive reenforcement has advantages over the traditional negative approach. A positive attitude in teaching does not condone problems which need attention or correction; it is simply a way to identify the solution to a problem without sacrificing the student's self-esteem. The goals of a program and their importance and desirability are not comprised in a positive teaching environment; to the contrary, they are usually supported or heightened. Such a technique encourages the application of solutions to problems in place of invective criticism directed toward the unfortunate student thus singled out. The objective is to avoid the reaction of anger or resentment and replace it with energy applied to the solution of the problem and a continued respect for the goal.

GOALS FOR PERFORMING ENSEMBLES IN TRAINING

Common agreement on the goals of performing ensembles at the various levels of junior and senior high school is far from unanimous. Some difference in purpose and objective is certainly justifiable and understandable because of the variety of band programs in existence. In general, it is not difficult to identify the difference in goals between a training ensemble and one whose chief purpose is performance of band literature. Bands which evolve in limited enrollment find the need to continue the study of technical skills while also continuing the performance of band literature at an appropriate level. Larger band programs with the luxury of more students and private instructors can establish separate bands of certain grade levels which maintain a natural progression of skills from one performance level to the next.

The point of least agreement is possibly rooted in the philosophy of *how well* the literature should be performed by groups at any level.

The dramatic growth of festivals, contests, and "super contests" have expanded the opportunity for bands to prove just how well they really can perform a given selection or program. As might be expected, this has produced at least two divergent groups with differing opinions about the amount of time which can justifiably be devoted to performance preparation, particularly for competition. At one extreme are bands which perform at the highest professional standard of musical competence. The opposing view points to such performances as overconcentration on limited literature at the expense of the student. Certainly it is difficult to be critical of a superior performance. High achievement is a goal of the American way. The democratic process encourages complete freedom to become the best.

The solution to this disagreement is not likely to be the solution to the real problem of bands and music in our country. This raises instead, the question of whether or not *anyone* is really teaching music through the medium of the performing ensemble in the public schools.

Performance-Based Objectives for Discipline

Somewhere we must find a middle ground upon which to base a rational and daily approach to performance for bands. Keep in mind that the standards of discipline that we have a right to expect from students must relate directly to the achievement of the goals. There will be some positive correlation between the levels of achievement in performance and the discipline which the demands of the program may impose upon the students and they upon themselves.

With the foregoing acknowledgement of differing opinions, the following specific goals for performing ensembles would seem characteristic:

1. Technical advancement which permits improved performance through:
   a. improved reading skills
   b. improved technical skills which assist the student in playing music of various musical periods and style, using correct spacing, articulation, dynamic levels, and instrumentation
2. Musical objectives through:
   a. study of literature which illustrates form such as the march, overture, suite, symphonic poem, and symphony
   b. study of style and period including transcriptions which illustrate baroque, classical, romantic, and contemporary

3. Performance for school and community including:
   a. athletic events, school assemblies, special holiday music, pep rallies, and formal concerts
   b. civic events such as parades, dedications, special days, and civic club entertainment
4. Contest and festival participation for marching and concert including:
   a. traditional "district" or "region" festivals, or rated contests, performing music often prescribed from a graded or selected list
5. Individual student participation through:
   a. solo and ensemble participation
   b. individual competition for select or honor groups
   c. regional or national music award competition
   d. summer music camp participation

This list may or may not be characteristic for a given program or philosophy but it includes at least some, if not many, goals which band directors encounter or originate for their programs. It is important to remember that in order for discipline and achievement to grow and to work, the director and his students must conceive these as *worthwhile* goals and identifiable progress *must* be apparent. Any time that either of these conditions change or become in doubt we can expect a discipline problem to develop.

Differences in Goal Perception

It is safe to assume that not all members of a performing ensemble share the aesthetic desires of their director. Dealing with potential problems in order of magnitude, there will always be a few students who must be separated from the group because they do not share the desire for achievement and are serving to deter others from the established goals. A more complete treatment of this problem is covered in the section on policy, but to be sure, such students must be separated from the group.

Appeal of Band as an Activity

Yet another group within the band will only partially embrace the goals which have been established. The effort from these students will fluctuate in intensity according to their perception of the importance of the particular objective in which the ensemble is involved. These students love and support outdoor and athletic-support activities; marching band will have a high priority in their willingness to give energy to the objective. Thank God for this segment of the band! They will lend support to the single phase of the band program which attracts more attention than any other. They will support the performance goal which is seen by more school and community patrons than all of the other events combined. The support engendered by the marching band often keeps the double reeds in the annual budget.

Band for a Love of Performance

A third group of perhaps lesser numbers will be those students who have a diminished enthusiasm for the activities of outdoors and marching band. Their preference lies rather in the desire for musical achievement on the instrument which relates in a direct way to more serious and challenging music of the concert band. Again, a blessing! These students do not openly withdraw their support from certain goals of the program but tolerate them in anticipation of their real interest when they can become more intensely involved in the state of the art.

You can see that there exists a diversity of heterogeneous interests in support of the goals of the band program. Such diversity can easily become fragmented to the extent of partial or even total dissolution of the discipline required to channel individual efforts and appropriate acts in correct sequence toward the achievement of objectives. Herein lies the role of the director, the music specialist, the rule maker, the judge, the musician, the motivator, and finally, the master of emotions and skills which must be developed into a band for all purposes.

FORMULATING BAND POLICY

The formulation of a book on band policy is an integral part of the overall plan for an effective band program. Such a collection of information is usually referred to as a "handbook" and is prepared for distribution to each student and parent connected with the band program. The purpose is to provide, in summary form, important information about the purpose and administration of the program. Certain areas will only be covered in a general way, while some others will be dealt with quite specifically. The handbook is not intended to be a curriculum guide, but it should include general information about the scope and objectives of the program as well as specific details of student involvement, participation, and behavior. The following outline of a band policy handbook is suggested:

1. Philosophy and Goals
   a. Music as an important element in the quality of life.
   b. How music enriches the traditional curriculum with opportunities for self-expression, creativity, and social and emotional development.
   c. Realization of goals through learning to play an instrument.
   d. All students have the right to pursue an interest in music.
2. Scope and Purpose
   a. Teach the student to play a musical instrument with full musical understanding.
   b. Provide participation in musically satisfying performing ensembles.
   c. Provide competent instruction for graded levels of achievement.
3. Performance Opportunities and Requirements
   a. Performing ensembles: marching band, concert band, wind ensemble, jazz band, solo and small ensembles.
   b. Summary of individual standards of achievement and how these relate to standards for large ensembles.
   c. A general schedule of yearly activities and participation requirements.
   d. Scholastic eligibility.
4. Standards of Behavior
   a. The importance of disipline and the need for self-discipline.
   b. The students' responsibility to school and community.
   c. Attendance policy and requirements for rehearsals, performances, and trips.
   d. Penalties for violation of policies.
5. Rewards
   a. Grading policies.
   b. Promotion. Requirements for membership in advanced or more select/mature bands.
   c. Band awards. Qualifications for jackets, letters, and emblems.
   d. Annual recognition banquets and annual band trips.

6. Band Support Groups
   a. Band booster clubs.
   b. Civic and community support groups.
7. Opportunities for Leadership
   a. Student Officers.
      (1) Drum Major
      (2) Assistant Drum Major
      (3) Band Officers
   b. Band Council.
   c. Band Staff.
      (1) Wardrobe
      (2) Library
      (3) Equipment
8. Administrative Procedures
   a. Enrollment costs and fees.
   b. Instrument and equipment policies, and responsibilities.
   c. Attendance policies (The parents' responsibility in providing supporting information for excusing absences.)
   d. Scheduling private instruction.

The outline above can be easily altered or expanded to meet the needs of the individual director or band program. When originating such a handbook policy, an important determination must be made regarding the involvement of the school administration and the students. It goes without saying that band policies must exist within the framework of general school policies. Often such a general policy book for the school system is available and should be carefully studied. The band policy book will become an extension which is based on school policy but expanded to fit the specialized needs of the band program. Particularly important is establishing agreement between these two documents on matters of behavior, discipline, and penalties. Matters dealing with expulsion from band, probation for misbehavior, and rules concerning the use of tobacco, drugs, and alcohol must be very carefully defined and understood between parents, students, and the school. The policy on scholastic eligibility is usually defined by the state as well as the school, and must be correctly interpreted for the parent and student.

In addition to the agreement and support of general school policies, a second important concern is student involvement in defining band policy. In certain circumstances, a policy handbook can be written almost exclusively by the band director with full confidence that it will be accepted by both parents and students. Such a director may be of long and respected tenure within the school and community and his word and judgment easily accepted, but it is more likely that such a project should be the product of cooperative effort between director and students. It is not uncommon to involve students in the act of handbook preparation. The number invited or elected to take part should be limited. The areas for student input must be carefully defined. Several of the topics in the outline would be appropriate for student participation. The overall structure of the band program and philosophical precepts are usually predetermined. It is not unusual, however, for a director to gain considerable insight from student reaction to such matters which can, in turn, be applied to treatment of the subject.

Typical Areas of Student Concern

Areas where students may feel a greater concern would be in the policy matters of attendance, behavior, grading, awards, and penalties for policy violation. When considering these matters, it is best to isolate the students' attention to one or two subjects at a time. A suggested plan can be presented by the director for study and reaction by the students at a subsequent meeting. This provides the opportunity for outside discussion away from the control or influence of the director which may be inhibitive. During such a period of planning and policy formulation, it is entirely appropriate to report to the rest of the students on a regular basis since the final results will eventually be of concern to all.

The final product of handbook planning should be a concise but adequate statement of facts and information which speaks for the values and strengths in a band program. It should be a document which the director feels comfortable in handing to the school principal, counselor, or each new student. It should be shared with each parent of a new beginning band member, as well as the parents of older students at the first yearly meeting of the band boosters' organization.

THE OUTLINE REVIEWED

Statement of Philosophy

The opening statement of philosophy must reflect the honest position of the director/teacher. These are not words which should be copied from another source unless they reflect true feelings and motivation They should be words which continue to have relevant meaning when the budget cuts threaten the program or when the school board or administrative decisions fall the wrong way.

Scope and Purpose in the Classroom

In developing the "Scope and Purpose" section a director must continue to relate to the real situation which exists within the classroom, concert stage, or marching field. Parents and patrons reading this section must develop an insight into the real working events of what may be totally foreign to their concepts of the band program.

Performance Opportunities and Requirements

A description of the performance opportunities and requirements should begin to transmit an awareness of responsibility by the parent and the student. An important lesson to be gained from the band program is the importance of the individual to the success of the group. This is the principle of teamwork whereby all of the members of the ensemble sacrifice certain inconveniences to achieve a goal.

Guidelines for Student Behavior

The fourth section of the outline dealing with "Standards of Behavior" is one that may be treated in some detail. This could well be the only written record of a director/teacher's position in resolving certain emotional issues, for it is a rare occasion when parents can adopt a truly objective position dealing with penalties inflicted upon their own children. No teacher should be reluctant to adopt a position for the enforcement of standards of behavior. Unpleasant tasks such as the discovery of students using drugs or alcohol in connection with band activities require a calm but firm response from the director. Each member of a family so affected must be treated with respect, but such problems must be pursued expediently and fairly. When the consequences of such an eventuality are spelled out for all to see, the director is protected, as is the integrity of the policy and the band program.

Grading and Evaluation

Section 5. covering "Rewards" is also one which can be of a controversial nature. Grading policies in support of superior band ensemble achievement can be more stringent and demanding than academic classes in the same school system. Parents and students may feel it is their right to call such matters into question, even when the standards are clearly spelled out. It is important to explain the relationship of such grading policies to the achievement of goals and objectives. This policy may produce the first occasion in the school life of a student when the grade is the result of good achievement rather than good intentions or polite behavior.

As a general guideline, grades must relate to performance assessed on an individual basis. Such evaluation can be extremely burdensome and time consuming when requiring students to play off weekly or biweekly assignments. However, if such assignments are meaningful they will contribute immeasurably to the success of the program. Examples of productive individual playing requirements are:

1. Early summer: Playing technique and development studies.

2. Early fall: Memorization of marching performance music.

3. Early winter: Scales and rudiments for district or region "select" band tryouts. Normally all students are not involved in such individual competition, but certainly scales and rudiments, which are only a part of the required procedure, may be considered a desirable goal for all instrumentalists.

4. Midwinter: Specific assignments of band literature for concert band placement and seating auditions. The literature should be planned for concert performance and thus contribute to the achievement of a goal.

5. Spring: Technique and tonal development studies. Concert contest performance literature. Promotion requirements for the next level of performing group.

Most other criteria for rewards are easily defined and student involvement is normally desirable.

Outside Support

A few brief paragraphs outlining the structure and functional purpose of band support groups is normally all that is needed. A summary of the meeting schedule, the structure of officers and how they are elected, and the relationship of the school and outside groups should be included.

Student Development

An important part of band activity is the provision for leadership development. A band council has an important role for self-government which provides valuable experience in training. Opportunities to function as an officer or staff member provide some very practical experience for developing responsibility and skills in working with others.

Administrative Detail

Administrative procedures should be detailed regarding cost and any fees required. A brief statement of the need for such policy and how the money is used to support the program must be included. The responsibility of the student in caring for a school-owned instrument and uniform should be detailed. This is especially important since school districts seldom carry insurance against damage or loss. Frequently individual family homeowners insurance will cover such liabilities, but these responsibilities must be set forth. The school's responsibilities for student liability (or lack of it) in band travel may be included in this section.

Keeping Students and Parents Involved

In many schools where there is no provision for printing or a budget for such, the typing and assembly of the completed handbook may become a project of the band council or parents. Again, such involvement is a healthy contribution to the success of the band program; it is one way to assure interest and publicity in the completion of this important feature of band organization and planning.

BIBLIOGRAPHY

Bollinger, Donald E. *Band Director's Complete Handbook.* (West Nyack, NY: Parker Publishing Company, 1979)

Green, Eddie. *Bulletin: Making the Music Classroom a More Inviting Place to Learn.* (Elkhart, IN: The Selmer Company, 1981)

Hovey, Nilo W. *Efficient Rehearsal Procedure for School Bands.* (Melville, NY: Belwin-Mills Publishing Corporation, 1981)

Hunter, Madeline. *Mastery Teaching.* (El Segundo, CA: TIP Publications, 1982)

Kruth, Edwin C. "Motivation, Practice, Adjudication." (Kenosha, WI: G. Leblanc Corporation, nd)

7

Analyzing the Sound
of Wind Groups

A major concern for directors whose responsibilities include the rehearsal of the concert band is the analysis of sounds heard on the podium. The physiological conditions of hearing sounds are not exactly the same for any two people. Certain limits develop within the human ear which precludes one person hearing sound exactly like the next. Conditions such as age and hearing damage in younger people influence the limits of the frequencies which are normally transmitted to the human sensory apparatus. In addition, the varied conditions surrounding a director's history and background for assimilating sounds must be recognized. Such an array of variables makes it most unlikely that inexperienced directors will be able to correctly hear and analyze the sound of wind groups at first.

A difficulty with listening skills may often be attributed to the director and former student who has emerged from a performing experience in a small and poorly trained school ensemble. However, such an individual is often no more limited than one whose experience was gained in a large and superior group. The student in either circumstance was not listening to the band from a vantage point of the podium; nor was he listening for the purpose of assimilating and rehearsing all of the sounds in the room. Instead, his concentration was focused primarily on his own individual sound and its place in the section or peripheral ensemble.

CONCEPTS OF A CORRECT SOUND

How then does one go about the training of listening for, and hearing, correct ensemble structure? Whose concept of "correctness" should one accept? Within a short period of contest or festival experience, the new director will become sensitively attuned to such descriptives as bright, dark, brittle, dull, cloudy, and brilliant, among a host of other adjectives which may appear on his adjudication sheet after a contest performance. From such experiences and with the help of more mature directors, the gradual formulation of a "correct" concept of ensemble sound will begin to take shape. However, such a correct concept is not universal and what may be considered acceptable in one region or part of the country may be quite different from that of another. The final decision about a correct ensemble sound will be somewhat of an individual preference and not necessarily like that of another. This matter of judgment and preference falls within the freedom of the art of musical expression, and no effort to completely standardize the concept of band sound should be made here.

There are a number of limiting factors which influence the sound of the ensemble that must be discussed and understood. These considerations may be divided into three broad categories:

1. Size and instrumentation of the band
2. Grade and maturity of the individual
3. Experience and background of the individual

Size and Instrumentation in Development of Wind Bands

The possibility of variety in this category of conditions are virtually unlimited. Control of this factor is important from the outset in correctly instrumentating beginning band classes. Over the years of band history, an accepted or standardized instrumentation for various kinds of wind groups has gradually evolved. The three most common designations today are (1) the wind ensemble, (2) the concert band, and (3) the symphonic band.

The term "concert band" generally refers to the medium-sized group of the three listed. This particular playing unit seems to have emerged from the standard military bands of World Wars I and II which were originally patterned after the Regimental Bands of Britain. These military bands provided for approximately 28 musicians. Over a period of time, outside of the military influence, this number has been expanded to an "ideal" size of 60 to 70 players. (See Figure 7-1.) This "concert" or "full" band was enlarged with the advent of emphasis in performance at universities, and as such, became known as a "symphonic" band. (See Figure 7-2.) A group so designated usually had from 100 to 110 members with a significantly large number of woodwinds.

The most recent development in instrumentation is known as the "wind ensemble." This ensemble was originally a group of

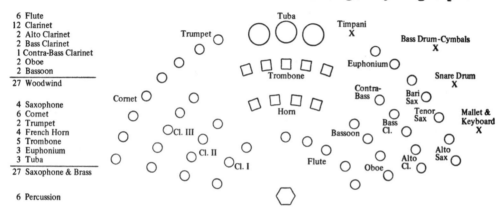

Figure 7-1 Concert Band Seating

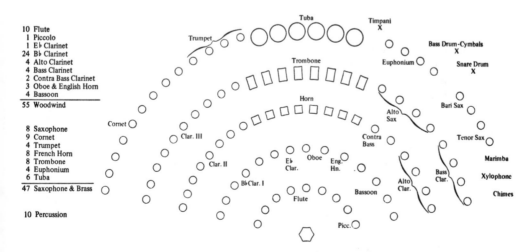

Figure 7-2 Symphonic Band Seating

approximately 37 winds plus percussion. The demand for percussion in contemporary band literature frequently requires an expanded percussion section thus bringing the wind ensemble of today up to a total of 44 to 46 players.

A comparative analysis of the three basic ensembles is shown in Figure 7-3. Let it be known from the outset that considerable variation in total size and instrumentation is dictated by the reality of the problems encountered in the public schools. In fact, many performing groups that are of "wind ensemble" dimensions survive in the functional role of the concert band. Perhaps it is only in ideal programs that we find the large symphonic band effectively performing appropriate literature, and within that unit also does the true wind ensemble take on its separate identity with its own literature.

Functional Roles.

The great majority of school bands in the United States continue to be functional groups that can adjust to the needs of both marching

	Wind Ensemble	Concert Band	Symphonic Band
Flute	2	6	10
Piccolo	1	(1)*	1
Eᵇ Clarinet	(1)*	(1)*	1
Bᵇ Clarinet	6	12	24
Alto Clarinet	(1)*	2	4
Bass Clarinet	1	2	4
Contra-Bass Clarinet	1	1	2
Oboe	2	2	2
English Horn	1	(1)*	1
Bassoon	2	2	4
Alto Saxophone	2	2	4
Tenor Saxophone	1	1	2
Baritone Saxophone	1	1	1
Cornet	4	6	9
Trumpet	2	2	4
French Horn	4	4	8
Trombone	2	4	6
Bass trombone	1	2	2
Baritone	2	3	4
Tuba	2	3	6
Percussion	5 to 8	5 to 10	6 to 10
	42 to 47	60 to 70	105 to 115

*Indicates possible doubling.

Figure 7–3. Instrumentation

and concert seasons. Many of these are both smaller and larger than the instrumentation shown, but the ratio of woodwinds to brasses must have some controlled logic. The demands of this group for marching purposes tend to dictate a larger brass and percussion section than would be considered ideal, but this must be taken into account when structuring the sound indoors.

The Woodwind Choir

The key to good balance is based upon the strength of the particular voice and the demand for multiple parts written for the section. The following summary of written part functions is provided as a guide for good instrumentation. Radical deviation in instrumentation often accounts for the structural problems which must be analyzed in rehearsal.

The flute is a light sound normally written in two parts. A minimum of two players per part is required. The function is frequently melodic. Separate parts, when provided, are in duet.

The B$^\flat$ clarinet originated its role from the string section of the orchestra and continues that function in band literature. Best clarinet section balance is obtained by adding greater numbers to parts in the lower register. Thus in a section of twelve, the distribution of three 1st, four 2nd, and five 3rd clarinets would be more satisfactory than an equal division of four players per part. This distribution recognizes the natural projection of the instrument when playing in the upper register. The bass and contra-bass clarinet are critical in completing the woodwind choir and one of each is much preferred over two of only one instrument.

The duplication of players on similar parts for double reeds works differently for the oboe and bassoon. Doubling on either the 1st or 2nd oboe part is not advisable; however, such practice is customary for the bassoon. The natural tuning problems inherent in the oboe are magnified by the timbre of the tone. The use of characteristic vibrato further compounds the problems of using more than one player on a part. The bassoon seems to react more favorably to the need for a blended sound when two are used on the same part.

The saxophone section is usually structured in quartets of two altos, one tenor, and one baritone. It is not unusual to hear bands with larger sections because of the popularity of the instrument in jazz and stage bands, as well as its effectiveness out of doors. The problem of greater numbers in the concert band is completely manageable although it is often necessary to employ muting devices or the use of only a portion of the section at a time.

The Brass Choir

Although the trumpet is by far the predominant instrument in use, the traditional labeling of parts is still for three "cornet" parts and less frequently, two "trumpet" parts. Pairs of players (either cornet or trumpet) are assigned to play "cornet" parts while one player (again, either cornet or trumpet) can usually handle each separate trumpet part.

French horns are normally assigned in quartets. The orchestral practice of writing first and third parts in a higher register than second and fourth parts is not common in band literature, and the players may be assigned, in numerical order, parts according to their skills or ability. When adding more horn players to the quartet, they should be added to the highest and lowest parts in that order; thus a section of six horns would have two players assigned to the 1st and 4th parts while one horn would play each of the 2nd and 3rd parts. This assignment would assume the availability of equal players; differing ability levels would dictate the doubling of other parts.

Trombones fare quite well with two players on each of the three parts. When more than six players are used they should be added to the 1st and 2nd parts since the bass trombone part is often reinforced in other voices.

The baritone and tuba sections, having but one part to play, require multiple players for best effect and balance. More than one player on each of these parts is always desirable in ensemble performance.

The Percussion Ensemble

The entire realm of percussion writing has expanded so rapidly that an adequate section is often difficult to predict. In addition to the usual requirements of four persons playing snare drum, bass drum, cymbals, and tympani, the addition of keyboards, traps, and other "skins" are now considered normal in band scoring. This fact, together with the demands for a variety of skills in marching percussion makes it necessary to plan for larger percussion sections.

Optional Instruments

The small concert band must omit the regular use of certain instruments which are not always required. These instruments can easily be mastered by other players in like sections and include piccolo, English horn, contra-bassoon, E♭ clarinet, alto clarinet, and

B^b soprano saxophone. Such voices are often doubled in other sections but should be available when scored.

The Wind Ensemble

The wind ensemble is a less flexible group in its basic instrumentation requirements. It was conceived as a group in which there would be an absolute minimum of doubling of parts. Thus the instrumentation is variable only according to the needs of the literature. The purpose and scope of the wind ensemble is less appplicable to the public school band program, although it must certainly be considered a viable unit in the band movement. Its musical function cannot be replaced or substituted in certain compositions, and those who realize the musical worth of the wind ensemble do so because they understand its application to specific literature.

The Symphonic Band

The large symphonic band has enjoyed a vigorous growth throughout the 1960's and early 1970's. As band programs grew larger, the symphonic band proved to be an ideal vehicle to accommodate greater numbers of skilled players. It complimented the pattern of growth in the marching band which has come to value its effectiveness in terms of volume and power. The concept of expanded instrumentation in the symphonic band can be educationally justified since it can serve more students from the same base of organization. The available store of band literature, including transcriptions, seems to fit the large band concept quite well. As we move on toward the close of the century it will be interesting to note the direction and pattern of ensemble development. Signs of change and flexibility are occurring with regularity and only history will properly record the new directions.

Regardless of the size of the performing unit, certain requirements must be anticipated. All of the separate parts written into the musical score must be represented in performance although occasions arise when an oboe solo must be performed by muted trumpet, flute, or clarinet; such a practice need not inhibit musical results. The sounds of the chord must be present. The basic voices of the brass and woodwind choirs must be intact. While certain performances can tolerate minimal absence of bassoon, bass clarinet, or baritone saxophone, they will not long survive the absence of the tuba.

Large numbers of soprano voices like the flute, clarinet, and trumpet will make a band overly brilliant and top-heavy. Small French horn, trombone, and baritone sections weaken the sonority and richness of the band, often contributing to a bright quality even though the upper voices are staffed within reasonable limits. Large percussion sections including two or more snare drums playing at once make the band sound harsh and unmusical. Extreme care and judgment must be used in controlling the sound of a band in which several of the sections are numerically over- or understaffed.

Grade and Maturity

Students in the formative years of grades six through nine often reflect characteristics which influence the band sound. Some of these students may still be concerned with basic posture, embouchure, breathing, and hand position. Some have not yet learned to properly manage the instrument or music materials.

Minimum Expectations

The base line of what to expect from groups in this category starts with a sustained sound which is of good quality and characteristic of the instrument. Students in their second year of playing experience should have a good playing range extending up through the C above the staff for clarinets, and G above the staff for cornets or trumpets. These sounds should respond freely. The students should be able to articulate correctly three basic styles of tonguing: staccato, normally separated, and a smooth legato. The limit of articulation velocity will be 16th notes in pairs at a tempo not to exceed 120 beats per minute; four 16th notes at that tempo would likely produce problems.

Third- and Fourth-Year Development

The basic ensemble quality for students starting their third and fourth year of playing experience should be acceptably good. Problems for this group as well as for younger students begin to develop when extending facility and technique. Concentration on the motor skill of moving the tongue or fingers faster frequently requires a reminder and reinforcement of embouchure control and breathing habits. Rhythmic accuracy, especially accurate subdivision, must be constantly emphasized.

Fifth- and Sixth-Year Development

Those students who approach their fifth and sixth year of playing should more likely be dealing with problems of improper execution, and interpretation of style and dynamic control. Adjusting the note length as it relates to style continues to cause problems for high school students. Reminders of the importance of breath control and support in changing articulation patterns will always be necessary. Phrase lines will be broken or misemphasized. Musical concepts must continually be taught and reviewed.

Experience and Background

Unfortunately students of all ages frequently find themselves needing to make a musical contribution to a group without the proper musical experience or background. This problem is far less likely to happen in a well-organized program of sufficient size to provide for a graded performing ensemble, but this condition omits perhaps a majority of small-school music programs which fail to establish continuity because of a change of directors or poor teaching. Under these circumstances students tend to get older but not musically wiser, and are forced to become a part of a group for which the director has more ambitious musical standards.

Poor Rehearsal Discipline

Conditions within this category are characterized by the student who fails to respond to a basic conducting gesture such as the downbeat. Individuals play after the beat on slow passages, rush within the measures of technical difficulty, and fail consistently to subdivide the beat accurately. These students do not react with appropriate dynamics to differing size of conducting patterns and cannot relate to musical style such as legato and marcato. Poor rehearsal discipline is evident in failure to release the end of a phrase with the conductor or the band.

Continuity in the routine of a rehearsal is frequently interrupted by such students who are inattentive or slow to find a specified measure or rehearsal number. They have difficulty in knowing how much sound to produce to balance within the section at varying dynamic levels. There is no concept of musical line and the relative strength of notes in it. There is a lack of ability to discriminate dynamic levels between melody, harmony, or repetitive accompanying figures. These students are unable to match pitch or quality with other solo or ensemble sounds.

SUMMING UP

In summary, the director is faced with a typical teaching task in which fundamental habits of playing must constantly be reviewed and taught, as well as the end result of a satisfactory performance goal. Like any skilled professional, he is faced with the need to assess a given situation and immediately identify the problems. The sound which comes to the director on the podium is the only means by which music can be made. The flaws and faults all have rational explanation. The problems all have solutions.

BIBLIOGRAPHY

Duvall, Clyde W. *The High School Band Director's Handbook.* (Englewood Cliffs, NJ: Prentice-Hall, 1960)

Hovey, Nilo W. "Interpretation in School Band Performance." *Selmer Bandwagon.* (Elkhart, IN: The Selmer Company, 1962)

McBeth, W. Francis. *Effective Performance of Band Music.* (San Antonio, TX: Southern Music Company, 1972)

Neilson, James. "Rehearsal Techniques." (Kenosha, WI: G. Leblanc Corporation, 1962).

8

Teaching the Concert Band Sound

An attempt to describe something as complex as the concert or symphonic band sound can be approached only at the risk of being misunderstood. Writing words which produce a meaningful description of an aural concept is neither easy to do nor comprehend. There is, of course, not necessarily one "correct" band-sound concept. The endless variable characteristics of the band in real life produce many different possibilities of instrumentation, while ability and maturity levels also have a real effect on the final product. With all of this in mind it is still possible to define certain procedures and controls which apply to ensemble structure, regardless of size or other limiting factors.

THE PYRAMID DESIGN OF ENSEMBLE SOUND

The band, when structured in proper balance, can best be considered as a pyramid of voices arranged in general score order with the lowest frequencies representing the broad base of the pyramid . (See Figures 8-1 and 8-2.) At the outset, it is a little easier to visualize the separate wind choirs in such an arrangement, but the percussion ensemble as well as the full band must also be fitted into the order of this pyramid outline. The theoretical outline of such a group of balanced voices would actually be modified to a more trapezoidal form in which the top is only one-third the breadth of the base.

THE RELATIONSHIP OF REGISTER AND STRENGTH

There are actually two factors which categorize this arrangement of instruments when sounding in proper balance or strength. The placement in the pyramid is dictated first by the natural range of

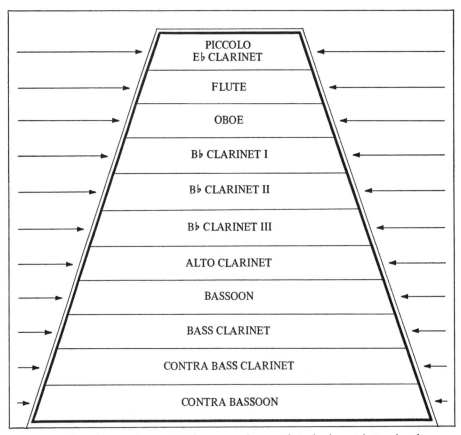

Figure 8-1 The pyramid concept for woodwinds shows the scale of diminishing effort required for balanced sound. Voices sounding successively higher frequencies require proportionately less effort to balance those below them.

frequencies which the instrument can produce, thereby placing the piccolo and flute at the top of the conceptual figure. This order continues on down through the separate choirs. The second factor in regulating band structure is that the prescribed or ideal strength in ensemble balance is almost exactly proportional to the location of that instrument in the pyramid to score order. In its simplest application, this explanation means that when the contra-bass clarinet is playing "fff," the piccolo would play only "f." When applying the same concept to the brass choir, the tuba would start the base of the figure and progress upward through the trumpet at the top. The saxophone family for purposes of teaching balance will more accurately fit with the brass choir. Application of this principle to percussion as well as some other exceptional factors will be discussed later.

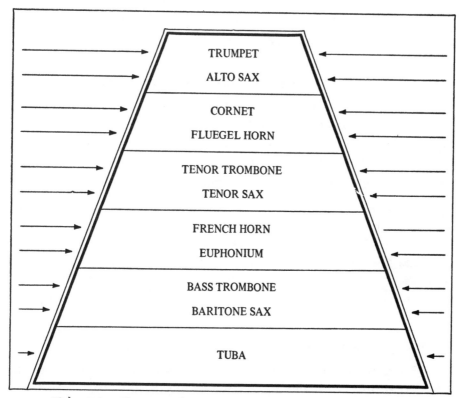

Figure 8-2 The pyramid concept for brass and saxophones shows the scale of diminishing effort required for balanced sound. Voices sounding successively higher frequencies require proportionately less effort to balance those below them.

It is appropriate to note here that the discussion in this chapter is based on the kind of sound most appropriate for the concert or symphonic band rather than the wind ensemble. Certain techniques may well be applicable to all three groups; however, the reader should understand that the frame of reference will always be the concept of the concert *band*. In terms of sound, the effect achieved by multiple instruments, such as clarinets playing single lines, is the distinguishing characteristic of the band. It is also entirely possible to achieve a complete or symphonic band sound without the color instruments such as piccolo, oboe, English horn, E^b soprano and alto clarinets, and also sometimes, the contra-bass clarinet. The principles of balance which are described will apply equally well to bands of 48 players as well as those of 110.

DEFINING AND ACHIEVING THE CONCERT BAND SOUND

These elements contribute most to the "complete" or concert band sound:

1. A blend of individual voices within instrument families.
2. A balance between individuals *within* sections and *between* other sections of the band.
3. Tone quality reasonably characteristic of the instrument from a majority of the members of each section.
4. Accurate intonation throughout the band.

These elements which are so important to the band sound should not be considered separate or isolated problems in rehearsal. They should be a part of the daily teaching procedure for all groups past the beginner level. The idea that tuning or the assessment of balance can wait until "after we play a few days," "after the kids get their lips back," or "after marching season" only serves to compound the problems and make them more difficult to solve.

Warm-Up Objectives

Every rehearsal period should begin with a "warm-up," during which training in the elements listed can be emphasized. This period in a rehearsal can be as brief as six minutes or as long as the entire period, but it should accomplish the following:

1. Allow the muscles of the arms, hands, and mouth to function actively without stress.

2. Provide an opportunity to "set" the breath to sustain tones or phrases of at least 16 counts in length at 72—80 beats per minute.

3. Provide a comparative listening opportunity during which the student may adjust his pitch mechanically and his hearing mentally. The director is provided the opportunity to begin listening critically.

It is during this period of time at the beginning of the rehearsal that much successful teaching begins to take place. The enormous responsibilities of the director/teacher suddenly begin to materialize. The director must be prepared to listen for, hear, and correct the following problems when stepping onto the podium to direct the first organized sounds of a rehearsal:

1. A predesignated dynamic level
2. The taking of the breath as if in rhythm with a fast "and" of the preparatory beat
3. Response to the baton on the initial attack
4. Quality of the attack and the ensuing tone
5. Duration of each note and length of the phrase, even (no, especially!) when playing a scale
6. The balance of voices *within* the section and *between* sections (This is the time to encourage the weaker players to match the level of the stronger ones. Mature players should not be permitted to overplay the dynamic levels.)
7. Correction of posture and instrument position as they affect the sound and pitch of the band

This list of responsibilities for the director must translate easily into goal-support activities which the students can understand. It may be helpful to address them individually:

The predesignation of dynamic levels for any routine activity, such as scale warm-up, is absolutely mandatory if the objective ability to play a 16-count phrase is ever to be achieved. Successful performance of music demands the physical ability to sustain note values for specific periods of time in order to make musical sense. The 16-count requirement set forth in the second warm-up goal will not be easily achieved by such instruments as flute and tuba; for them, it may need to be shortened to 8 or 12 counts followed by rests. However, by designating the dynamic level at "mf" for this exercise, the director immediately reduces the problems of overblowing and of balance. This kind of control, along with the objectives of sustained phrasing, is part of a realistic performance goal.

Taking the breath in rhythm is simply a disciplined approach to the formation of regular deep-breathing habits. Taking air in more quickly reinforces a natural inclination to compress more air in reserve. Students can hear each other performing this important preparatory act, and the director can be assured that it is happening. This breathing exercise in preparation for music at faster tempos can be lengthened to take up an entire beat. The difference in overall tone quality for a band which breathes properly will be obvious.

Insistence on *response to the baton on the initial attack* generally serves notice that it is time for the band to go to work as a unit. Total response by the band is, of course, the objective. Total response requires the solution to a host of other organizational problems that ultimately must bring a student to the rehearsal room, seated with all necessary equipment, and ready to concentrate on the improvement of his playing for a given period of time. The director who gives a downbeat without the full attention and participation of the band is merely continuing a problem which often accompanies the group to the concert stage. The decision about response to the baton must be made as it relates to musical performance; neither rehearsal nor performance should be expected to begin without total commitment of the band.

Identifying *quality of the attack and the ensuing tone* becomes a matter for the trained listener. All of the things which have gone on in preparation are certainly important, but now we begin to deal with the commodity of music, sound itself. Most professionally trained teachers can identify a good sound and many of them can adequately prescribe solutions to poor tone or attacks when isolated with a single student in the studio, but we are asking something quite different from the director on the podium. We are asking this person, whose mind has already been clouded and frayed with a number of other concerns, to sort out the sounds coming toward the podium from dozens of different sources. The director must instantly recognize and locate the problems and prescribe the solutions. All these reactions must be accomplished without interrupting the flow and intensity of a well-organized rehearsal.

Attention to *the duration of each note and length of the phrase* continues to provide the opportunity to teach accuracy in attack and release that supports musical objectives. This is a chance to address releases between notes in various styles as well as the musical taper of notes at the end of the phrase. Above all, unity in an approach to the ensemble sound is critical. This moment is the time to dispel the myth that playing together is merely starting together.

Teaching correct concepts of *balance of voices within and between sections* is one of the paramount goals for the effective performance of band music. This challenge is more critical to band performances than any other group because of the effect of multiple voices playing the same musical line. This point in the rehearsal opens the opportunity for students sitting generally behind the source of the sound to react to advice from the director about its effect from in front. Playing and performing with good balance is a reaction from students who produce results they do not actually hear. The performers' sole contribution to good balance must be based on the advice from the director.

Almost as an afterthought, the *correction of posture and position* continues to be needed when this factor obviously effects the production and contribution of sound. Younger groups frequently need these reminders; older and more mature players almost certainly should not need them, but such reminders are occasionally appropriate even in college bands.

The immediate reaction to such a list of responsibilities is that no rehearsal can ever get beyond the first note. Such problems are so predominant in many bands that the rehearsal period could easily be spent correcting them to the complete neglect of other objectives. It is safe, however, to assume that the director cannot solve all of these problems at one time, and it now becomes a matter of judgment and skill as to which problems must be approached and to what degree they may be resolved at any given time.

Solving Problems in Rehearsal

It may be wise to first establish the fact that the solution, to a rather complete degree, for each of the problems described above is attainable for even an average school band. The teaching process then becomes a chain of events which might be outlined in the following manner.

At the beginning of a program of instruction designed to teach sound and structure to the band, the director should not interrupt the particular playing activity each time a problem appears. The normal approach would be to complete the scale or passage and then stop to identify the problem. The solution should be offered and immediately applied. An exception to this approach will be the case where this process of identification with accompanying solution has been applied without success; then it is reasonable to assume that the solution is not working because (1) it is the wrong solution, or (2) it has not been given time and repetition to work, or (3) the student never understood the identity of the problem. When the solution seems to be ineffective, it is imperative to interrupt the flow of the rehearsal to find out which of the conditions exist and how to alter them.

As a rule, some constructive activity toward a given problem should continue until a degree of progress is recognized. This activity may be nothing more than identifying the problem at first. Later it will continue as actual improvement in sound is heard until finally it is resolved to the satisfaction of the director. Improvement does not mean that the problem will never again surface, and hence, does not absolve the director of further responsibility to hear and identify it. It simply means that he has achieved some progress to keep the group from sliding back in one area while the next one is approached. The teaching procedure might be summarized in the following steps:

1. The director hears and identifies the problem.
2. The director makes a decision as to when to address the problem, stopping the band for that purpose.
3. The problem is explained and the solution proposed.
4. The solution is applied and given time to work by repetition, as needed.
5. Failure is analyzed or success is reinforced.
6. The director continues to listen for recurrence of the problem while proceeding on to others.

Effective Tools for the Warm-up

Many directors develop or adopt individualized techniques for the opening part of a band rehearsal. For directors who have not established a preference or who want to examine other possibilities, the following material is recommended:

The F concert scale. Preferred because of its two-octave potential for most brass players and the clarinet choir. Generally more stable than the B♭ concert scale for tuning purposes.

The scale should be performed from memory in the rhythm of whole notes for each scale tone with four such tones in one breath for a total of sixteen counts.

The rhythm can be varied later to simulate rhythmic problems that support performance goals.

Brass players who experience problems at first in starting on the low F beneath the staff may be accommodated by playing the scale in descending order from the middle of the two-octave spread.

The C concert scale. This scale tends to emphasize problems of tuning which are frequently neglected. It establishes the critical first and third valve combinations as the tonic note for trumpet, baritone, and tuba, and the equally troublesome sixth position for trombone. The scale is still easy to control for clarinets (starting "d" under the staff) and serves to anchor group pitch for brasses who invariably start the scale playing sharp. With a little experience, the group can arrive at a common pitch center on the third note of the scale as the ear begins to dictate tuning adjustments (either mechanical or physical) based on a correct interval of a major third.

Sixteen Chorales by J. S. Bach; arranged by M. Lake, published by Schirmer. This particular collection of chorales has set the standard for material of its kind. It is of medium difficulty and is useful to accomplish the following:

1. Correct balance of the separate woodwind and brass choirs
2. Unison and octave tuning in each of the four harmonic parts
3. Correct chord balance within sections as well as full band
4. Principles of music theory by identification of major and related minor keys
5. Phrasing, flexibility of tempo, release, attack, and all basic problems connected with the art of conducting.

BACK TO THE BASICS

Here are some useful suggestions in applying the techniques for achieving the four elements listed at the beginning of the chapter.

Blending Voices

Achieving a "blend" of individual voices within the same family of instruments is usually a matter of basic tone quality, but is not separated from the characteristics of intonation and balance. Sounds which have a rich and open fullness are characteristic of the flute, cornet, and baritone. The brass section sound which is heard in recordings of the Chicago Symphony, especially during the time that Philip Farkas was principal French horn, is a good example of the ideal. Sounds which seem pinched or are produced with a great deal of stress and tension will be difficult to blend or assimilate. A good "first step" toward this objective is to get all players in a section on the same brand of instrument and the same or similar mouthpiece. Students who have little or no flexibility of pitch without adjusting the instrument usually do not have good embouchure control. It will be difficult to change anything about their playing including the ability to blend their quality until that condition is changed.

"Inter-Sectional" and "Intra-Sectional" Balance in the Band

The problem of achieving balance between voices within the same section is often confused with poor blend. Establishing proper balance depends upon producing more or less sound. In the process of reducing the amount of sound produced in the upper register of the clarinet, the quality is often changed from an extremely strident tone to one that blends perfectly well. The opposite may also be true. An airy, dull sound in the lower register of the clarinet which is too weak for proper balance frequently turns into a characteristic clarinet sound when proper breath support is demanded. Thus the dual problem of blend and balance are resolved with the basic approach to characteristic tone quality.

Within a section of average and equal players, poor balance is usually a product of inexperience coupled with over- or under-exertion required for register extremes. First trumpet parts tend to be high, and are often misplayed loudly as a part of the effort expended by the individual. Establishing control in the upper register of all instruments is an important part of the art of correctly teaching the instruments. All of the winds offer the possibility of being played too loudly in the upper register unless some appreciation for balance is instilled by the director. Any given three-note chord in the clarinet or trumpet section must be adjusted with stronger volume levels from the 2nd and 3rd parts. The correct concept of balance is more easily taught when basing the amount of sound required for the chord on the volume of the lowest note. The amount of sound required from the top voices is usually a third less than the lowest part in relation to the pyramid principle.

The relationship of energy expended to playing range is easily established in the warm-up exercises on scales. In the process of playing the F concert scale, the director is obligated to listen for equality of dynamics from the lowest to the highest note of the scale. It will become easy to pick out certain voices who deviate most severely from the predesignated dynamic level. More subtle differences within various sections can be diagnosed when isolating them for short periods of the warm-up sequence. An organized effort to hear the major sections of the band must be planned into the week-long sequence if a director is to make progress in teaching balance.

Balance Between Choirs

As balance begins to improve within instrument sections, the process of listening should be shifted to larger groups. The clarinet choir should establish its own identity of structured sound without the addition of saxophones or double reeds. The latter two groups may be combined with the French horns for purposes of practicing good balance although the oboe is best combined with other melodic voices such as the 1st cornet or trumpet, flute, and alto saxophone. The low-brass section must work to establish a balance identity of its own. The goal for this group, composed of trombone, baritone, and tuba, is to achieve a rich blend of strength and vitality. French horns conveniently fit into the same group but will tend to lose their identity; they will hear better when paired with the saxophone-double reed grouping.

Up to this point, the objective has been to group instruments with similar characteristics, but the end result will be groups of instruments that can achieve a balanced sound with any other set of voices of the band.

Understanding Structure Within the Percussion Ensemble

The percussion section must also achieve a concept of how balance applies to them. Exercises for this group are much more difficult to devise. This section is best treated separately because it reduces the ability of the winds to hear themselves when playing together. The principle of reinforcing the descending frequencies in the pyramid which applies to the winds does not work the same for percussion. The tympani or bass drum can easily dominate the sound of a full band as well as the total percussion section.

Classifying the Percussion Family

It is helpful to categorize the percussion section "skins" (correctly termed "membranophones") into two groups: Latin percussion and "regular" percussion. The voices in each group are capable of varying pitches from lowest to highest, much like the woodwind and brass choirs. In such a lineup of regular percussion the lowest pitch would be the large bass drum. The order would then proceed upward through the five tuned tympani, the roto-toms, and the snare drum. The Latin percussion family starts with the conga drum as the lowest voice and proceeds upward with timbales and bongos. A third family of "metal" instruments includes the tam-tam, suspended cymbal, and crash cymbals, in that order of basic pitch arrangement. The addition of wood block, tambourine, temple blocks, and other traps provides a host of sounds which are not easily categorized. The melodic percussion respond more nearly like melodic winds and can be controlled with a variety of mallets and playing skills.

The important point is to realize that the concept of balance applies also to all instruments of the percussion family. By recognizing some of the same standards of need for balance, and by applying the principles which are appropriate for the winds, the percussion section can become a vastly improved musical part of the band sound. The director must give this family of instruments the same attention as the winds, and he must work to apply listening skills which may be more difficult to acquire. Anyone who has adjudicated contest or festival events for bands has had the experience of hearing unbridled and raw percussion playing interfere with a musical performance. Such occasions range from an occasional cymbal crash of distracting proportions, to constant musical harrassment by the bass drum or tympani player. These problems of balance must be diagnosed from the podium, and the director must discipline his listening habits to include a standard of perspective between the percussion family and the two wind choirs.

Tone Quality Characteristic of the Instruments

The influence of tone quality on "blend" has already been mentioned. In addition to that consideration it must be recognized that the authenticity of the band medium is wholly predicated on the ability of the players to achieve a characteristic sound on their instrument. To expect a band sound to emerge with a section of buzzing or reedy clarinets is futile. Flutes that begin to whistle painfully in the high register or a brass section that produces a strident and pinched quality will never permit the band to achieve the sound which is desired. The importance of basic teaching is once again apparent. The ability of the teacher to produce or simulate characteristic tone quality on each instrument for the beginner looms ever more important in the success of the band program. When a lack of characteristic quality threatens the potential of the band, there is no choice but to immediately embark upon a course to repair or change embouchures, breathing, or anything else that may influence or improve the problem. Remedial teaching of this kind is most difficult but true success in musical expression is *impossible* without it.

SUMMING UP

Symphonic or concert sound becomes routine once the ensemble achieves the concept of it for several reasons. First, the director acquires listening skills which permit the immediate diagnosis of playing characteristics that have a negative effect on the sound of the band. Balance problems that occur from overblowing or improper tone production are immediately recognized and corrected. Second, the student members of such an ensemble accept their role in the structure of the band once they understand its purpose. They respond to the conditions around them, with the younger and inexperienced players accepting the pattern role of more advanced musicians. In such an environment the director does not have the task of constantly diagnosing and solving individual problems.

In reviewing the technique for establishing correct balance, it is best to start with the "section" or instrument family. The next step is to proceed to the separate choirs of woodwinds and brasses, not to overlook the percussion. The true symphonic band sound embraces an order of balance which permits a distinct contribution of each choir. In the woodwinds it begins with a very positive contra-bass, bass clarinet, and bassoon strength, proceeding upward through well-defined harmony parts in the clarinet section. It finally ends with a delicate but ever-so-important lyric flute quality clearly heard at the top. The conflict which often develops between the 1st clarinet and the flute has destroyed many a performance in the reversal of their relative strengths. These voices require constant scrutiny.

Similarly, the brass choir originates in the strength of the tuba, bass trombone, and baritone saxophone. From here, the two parts of the trombone section and baritone must be much in evidence before adding the carefully balanced cornet or trumpet section. The common practice of seating the trombones behind the trumpets often causes a balance problem that is easily corrected by changing the order of seating to place trombones in front. French horn balance will always pose a problem and may be assisted with advantageous seating near the front or outside of the band. Further reinforcement from the saxophone section is also helpful.

Melodic voices are often used as a measuring stick for comparing various families and bringing about unity. This set of voices can construct its own pyramid order from baritone, trumpet, alto sax, oboe, clarinet, and flute in ascending order.

Finally, it is well to remember that students will tend to produce a strength of sound that is convenient to them until they are properly advised about what is correct for the band.

BIBLIOGRAPHY

McBeth, W. Francis. *Effective Performance of Band Music*. (San Antonio TX: Southern Music Co., 1972)

Pizer, Russell A. *How to Improve the High School Band Sound*. (West Nyack, NY: Parker Publishing Company, 1972)

9

The Tuning Process

The entire realm of accurate intonation in the band is one of such magnitude that it must be treated in some detail. Exactly how a band manages to maintain accurate intonation has come to be viewed by many as the "mystery of the ages." The nonchalance with which this subject can be ignored by some directors until the week before a contest performance is a matter of repeated record. The fervent pleas from such directors to have a clinician come and apply the magic of correct tuning at a moment's notice is convincing evidence that the process is grossly misunderstood. The disheartening experience of watching a director stand in front of an electronic tuner and point dutifully at each and every wind player for a sample pitch which is then pronounced "sharp," "flat," or "okay" has been repeated too many times. Obviously, this is not the way bands learn to play in tune. A discussion of some techniques that work can be more helpful.

TWO PHASES IN SUCCESSFUL TUNING

The normal procedure for tuning the band is divided into two phases. The first phase details procedures which should be accomplished with isolated sections or families of instruments. The second phase is the continuing routine which must be used to whatever degree necessary in the daily rehearsals of the entire band. The entire tuning process is based on the premise that students can hear pitches at least as well as the director and once provided with the opportunity to identify a tuning problem, can apply the techniques for resolving it. The procedures which follow emphasize teaching students how to hear correctly tuned unisons and octaves.

Phase One: For Individual Sections or Families of Instruments

The first objective to be accomplished is proper adjustment of the actual length of the wind instruments. It is common knowledge that pitch becomes lower as the vibrating air column becomes longer. Much of the mystery of tuning for students can be eliminated with a clear preliminary explanation of this "longer and lower" principle. The initial phase of tuning is then a simple adjustment of the length of each wind instrument by means of the tuning slide, barrel, bocal, or actual extension of the instrument at its joints. The most appropriate note or group of notes to use for this adjustment represents an "average" pitch which best seems to accommodate the total instrument playing range. These "average" or tuning notes are given in Figure 9-1.

Controlling Temperature

In preparation for this procedure the director must insure that the student has adequately warmed up and that the instrument is warm and remains at a normal performance temperature. This is best done by insisting that the student be seated in the rehearsal room, go to an individual practice room, or any other regimented act which will permit him to warm up properly. If this is not possible, the warm-up process must be accomplished by the director before proceeding further.

Electronic Reference

It is only in this phase of tuning that the regular use of an electronic tuning device is recommended. In regular sequence, each member of the section should sound a given note to be checked for accuracy against the tuner. With a little practice the tuner can be eliminated in all but borderline cases, as a sounded tuning pitch is substituted for the meter or dial. Students should be encouraged to develop tonal memory for a specific pitch. The first line "E" is recommended for setting clarinet tuning with adjustment of only the barrel of the instrument. Some directors like to have students approach this pitch by playing the scale upwards to the note from the "C" below. Students who profit from such practice at first will soon learn to tune accurately without it. Once the "E" is set, each player should then proceed scalewise down to the "C" immediately below and check that tone with the tuner or another sound source. On some clarinets a compromise of adjustment may be necessary and should be made at this time, again only at the barrel joint. Next, the tuning accuracy of the "C" in the staff should be compared with the tuner or a correct pitch; usually only a slight adjustment is necessary that should be made between the first and second joints. Again, if the instrument is very sharp or flat on that pitch, a compromise will have to be made using the barrel joint.

A word of caution is appropriate here for the student who may experience considerable deviation from section pitch levels on this procedure. Such deviation would indicate the need for examination of the bore for obstructions, or length of the barrel. A nonstandard mouthpiece or a well-worn reed can likewise cause this problem. When the equipment appears to be in reasonable conformity, the embouchure or support technique of the student may be called into question.

Tuning to the Lowest Voice

Although the director is not encouraged to accept deviate levels of tuning it is always possible that a compromise may be necessary to accommodate the equipment of the strongest or first chair player who should eventually accept the responsibility for section tuning. Some well-known brands of clarinets are manufactured to lower pitch levels. A shorter barrel for such a player is a first possibility, but it is also possible that the entire section, and hence the entire band, may need to tune lower than one would normally choose.

Tuning Above 440

Under normal circumstances the band should initiate tuning at the A-440 level. This will provide most winds with some mechanical flexibility to tune accurately. Double reeds will often tend to play at a

Alto   Ten.

Flute. Pull as much as 1/4 inch if sharp on the majority of these pitches. Adjust other variations by rolling—changing direction of air stream. Check endplug with cleaning rod.

Clarinet. Control first three notes with barrel adjustment. Use tuning rings when pitch stabilizes. Pull up to 1/8 inch at middle joint to control C in the staff.

Saxophone. The Bᵇ concert is as good as any tone for alto and baritone. The tenor stabilizes well with a compromise between the F and Bᵇ concert pitches.

Oboe. Usually sharp on high F. Tuning for oboe is as much a listening exercise as a tuning adjustment.

Bassoon. Universally sharp on F. The joints can be elongated as well as pulling the bocal.

Cornet/Trumpet. The F concert is generally more stable, but the Bᵇ concert must also be tuned.

Figure 9-1   Notes for length adjustment.

French Horn. Second line G is good for F horn; third line C is a good starting tone for the B♭ side.

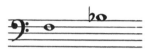

Trombone. The F in the staff is most stable and B♭ is almost as good. D above the staff is universally flat and the F above is sharp when the rest of the horn is tuned with closed slide.

Baritone. Same principle as cornet/trumpet.

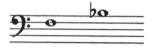

Tuba. Same principle as cornet/trumpet.

Figure 9–1. *(continued)*

slightly higher level, but they must be assisted in choosing reeds and bocals which permit them to attain 440. The importance of starting wind tuning at this level is critical because of the natural tendency of the pitch to rise during performance. Fortunately most of the winds respond in a similar fashion although an increase in internal instrument temperature seems to effect woodwinds more than brasses. Some experimentation with individual bands is necessary to determine the wisdom of retuning during a performance back to the original level. In some cases it may be best to let the performance continue at a level of 441 or 442.

Cornet or trumpet, trombone, baritone, and tuba section tuning can be treated in a similar manner with adjustment of the "F" concert (in the staff for cornet/trumpet, trombone, and baritone) made first and then the B♭ above it.

Tuning the Entire Playing Range

Once the initial adjustment of the instrument has been made in comparison to the tuner, various problem notes of an entire scale should be explored. All students should eventually be responsible for the assessment of any problems in the entire playing range of their instrument against the tuner. Many teachers prescribe the preparation of a chart of tuning deviation from each note on the student's instrument as a permanent reference. Such thoroughness takes any doubt out of the student's responsibility for playing the instrument in tune; however, the process needs to be repeated with some regularity since a student will change with maturity. At this point the student should be ready to make a substantial contribution to the band which plays in tune. The determining factor however, still lies in the hands of the skilled director/teacher.

Phase Two: For the Entire Band

This phase of tuning should normally be a part of the regular rehearsal routine. The period of time devoted to tuning, whether six minutes or more, cannot be isolated from the problems which continue to affect basic tone production, and the director will continue to guide and dictate breath support, embouchure tension, and dynamic levels.

An adequate warm-up period is still required as before when tuning was begun within the section. Careful supervision is necessary when first initiating a regimented warm-up and tuning procedure. As the students begin to adapt to the regimen and see the results, considerable responsibility in preparation for the beginning of the rehearsal can be left to their initiative.

Use of the Tuning Group in Ensemble Tuning

The first step in correct band tuning is the establishment of tuning groups. This procedure continues to function on the premise that (1) it is easier to hear and identify problems when tuning unisons and octaves, and (2) that students have the skills to resolve tuning differences once they are identified.

Representative Voices for a Common Pitch Center

The purpose in establishing a tuning group is (1) to start with a small number of voices which can easily resolve differences thereby setting a pitch standard for both themselves and the rest of the band, and (2) to match pitch from members of different choirs and families of the band to insure a standard pitch center once each player has had a chance to adjust his tuning.

A typical tuning group would be the first clarinet, first cornet or trumpet, and first alto saxophone. This group includes members of the two largest sections in the band who also represent the top voices of the woodwind and brass choirs. Their pitch and tone quality are in a register which is easily heard and discriminated by the human ear. These two voices are matched with the alto saxophone who is in reality not a member of either choir and represents the "rest of the band." In the beginning, this group should play an entire scale such as the F concert with clarinet and cornet starting on the middle "G." As they make adjustments to match all of the pitches in the scale, additional voices can prepare to enter the exercise. These voices usually include the first chair players from other sections who will enter one or two at a time. As this routine is expanded it will include more players, such as the "first" player on each of the different clarinet and cornet or trumpet section parts, and similar additions from all sections. Eventually the band should be equally divided so they can alternate in comparing pitches.

Developing Skill in Comparative Listening

The objective throughout the tuning procedure is to give students a comparative listening opportunity. Only as they have the chance to hear tuning problems will they acquire the skills to solve them. Rehearsals should be planned over a six-week period with a specified amount of time allotted to tuning exercises. A typical plan might include at least one longer period of concentration of as much as 30 minutes per week with shorter periods of 5 to 10 minutes allotted on other days. A person who truly desires to make this an effective process should record several sessions for analysis to note results or failure.

A variety of exercises to stimulate improvement in band tuning should be scheduled by the director. The use of an electronic tuner is entirely appropriate at first. It is not uncommon for both director and students to lose the reference pitch during a series of exercises. As listening skills and habits improve, the electronic device can be discontinued completely and the tuning group will be used to set the pitch. The exercises should help to concentrate and stimulate careful listening and tonal memory for given pitches. Exercises such as isolating a student on a faulty pitch of a scale encourage interest and attention. As the band starts up the scale, the director may point to a student with the problem; the band then drops out to permit the single student to be heard alone. The abrupt change of involvement suddenly throws the entire band into an intense listening exercise.

Directing alternate groups on repeated scale tones also provides opportunities for listening and correcting tuning. Whatever the device may be, it should be used consistently until progress becomes evident over a reasonable period of time. The final exercise is to involve the entire band through a unison or octave progression of the scale. With the achievement of accurate tuning the director will begin to identify that unique core of quality present in the ensemble which serves as a reward for patient effort of all concerned.

Playing in Tune

Once the second phase in ensemble tuning can be accomplished in a brief period in conjunction with the warm-up, the band is ready to learn to play in tune during the rehearsal and eventual performance. A band and the director must accept the tuning procedure as a constant and continuing activity which is never neglected or eliminated from playing. It continues to be the director's responsibility to identify tuning problems throughout the rehearsal, and to suggest solutions if the student is not able to do so.

Tuning in rehearsal must have the same priority as teaching correct rhythm, dynamics, phrasing, technique, style, or any other important element of music. It will respond in direct relation to the skill and time which is applied to its improvement.

It may be noted that the many details of exactly how to play each instrument in tune are not treated here. At some point in the instructions of the student, a detailed procedure of individual mechanical adjustment and the influence of embouchure tension and breath control must be covered. Two publications which provide detailed information on this subject are *Intonation Manual for Wind Instruments* by Clarence Sawhill and Glenn Matthews, and *Tuning the School Band and Orchestra,* by Ralph Pottle.

BIBLIOGRAPHY

Hall, Jody C., and Earle L. Kent. *The Language of Musical Acoustics* (Elkhart, IN: C. G. Conn Limited, 1957)

Pearce, Wesley. *Intonation Studies for Band.* (Logan: Utah State University Press, 1977)

Pottle, Ralph R. *Tuning the School Band and Orchestra.* (Hammond, LA: Byron-Douglas Publications, 1962)

Sawhill, Clarence, and Glenn Matthews. *Intonation Manual for Wind Instruments.* (Hammond, LA: Byron-Douglas Publications, 1959)

10

Musical Expression
in Band Performance

It would seem that the formidable task of achieving the correct band sound with an ensemble of winds and percussion would assure the aspiring band director a substantial degree of success in the profession of conducting. As important as this phase of teaching bands to play music may be, it is in part only a technical goal which does not necessarily assure musical success. There are even some who would assert that the technique of teaching correct band sound without the paramount ingredient of musical expressiveness can only assure a certain ordered sterility.

It is safe to assume that a relatively small number of band conductors will ever approach the level of achievement of William Revelli, Mark Hindsley, or Clarence Sawhill, all of whom have demonstrated an absolute degree of success in achieving correct band structure and musical expression. The standards of band performance at any level must include the all-important results of musical expression, whether accomplished at the most basic level of elementary band literature or with the most skilled professional ensemble.

The achievement of musical expression in band performance, then, must include yet another set of objectives. It becomes even more difficult in defining these objectives, to say which ones go beyond the realm of the mechanical or technical, and which contribute most to artistic conclusions. In a sense, they all ultimately contribute to the art of music. The successful performance usually generates an emotional response in the listener. This response is stimulated by a performer who is able to transform basic mechanical actions into an expressive art form, again, through the addition of the critical factor of emotion. A vital part of the conductor's responsibility in making music is the creation and control of this "emotion factor" for both the performer and the listener. In most cases the composer has created the vehicle for artistic expression, but the conductor becomes the one who must regulate and inspire the medium.

ELEMENTS OF MUSICAL EXPRESSION

The band which has become consistent in producing the correct structure of sound must move on to this final set of requirements for a quality performance of band literature.

1. Correct style through the application of characteristic tempo, correct rhythm, and appropriate note length and weight for each tone.

2. Correct dynamic levels and application of the traditional expressive marking that dictate the kind and strength of each sound.

3. Control of the breath for the proper interpretation of each phrase to achieve the musical effect intended by the composer.

In the most basic language of teaching these objectives are more simply stated as (1) accuracy of note lengths and placement, (2) a set of contrasting dynamics, and (3) breath control in musical phrasing. As the discussion of these requirements continues, every effort will be made to relate them to the responsibilities of the director outlined in Chapter 9. The maturing band director must develop a definite relationship between those things heard in the organized environment of the rehearsal and the musical requirements for a successful performance.

Style

The element of style in performance is achieved by adjusting the length and weight of individual sounds. The determination of such length and weight in musical style is dictated by what was traditionally done at the time the music was composed. In the performance of music transcribed for band from other mediums, the character and mechanical nature of the original medium is critical to the success of a band performance of the composition. Any deviation from the musical style of the original work must be tempered with sound musical judgment for successful results.

A review of the four broad chronological periods in music history will touch upon the basic differences in style during the periods of (1) Baroque, (2) Classical, (3) Romantic, and (4) Contemporary ("modern") band writing. It is well to keep in mind the possibility for considerable confusion in understanding the Contemporary Period since there is a marked difference between music of living or 'contemporary' composers and those composers whose music is characterized by experimental or nontraditional harmonies and techniques. The great majority of music written for band in the last twenty years may be classified and interpreted as "Romantic" music, even though the composers live in what is called the Contemporary period in music history.

The Baroque Period

The Music of Bach and Handel

The Baroque period in music generally covered the years 1600 to 1750, and was characterized by such composers as Corelli, Frescobaldi, Purcell, and Vivaldi. However, the dominating influence of Bach and Handel over that period is much in evidence in band literature today. In order to understand the influence of style in the band performance of their music, at least some basic knowledge about these composers is essential. In addition, a generous exposure to the recorded or performed work in the original medium is an important part of any band director's training. A recording of the original version of the transcription and an original score is extremely helpful in achieving an authentic performance.

Johann Sebastian Bach, who lived from 1685 to 1750, was born in Germany. His musical training and experience were in the area of voice and violin, as well as harpsichord and organ.This background in part explains his interest in, and prolific production of, compositions for the keyboard, orchestra, and various solo instruments as well as the sacred choral works.

George Frederick Handel was born in 1685 and lived until 1759. He also was born in Germany but lived much of his life in England, much to the credit of English musical heritage. His musical training, in addition to harpsichord and organ, also included the violin, and interestingly enough, the oboe. This performing experience on the double reeds explains Handel's affinity for scoring large oboe sections into some of his works. Unlike Bach, whose life was spent in music of the church, Handel composed opera as well as oratorio. His interest and travel led him to write for the entire realm of musical expression available in Europe including the keyboard, orchestra, wind instrument ensembles, and various instrumental solos.

Popularity of Baroque Music in Band Literature

A survey of band publications listed in the *Band Music Guide* published by *The Instrumentalist* reveals numerous band arrangements and transcriptions of composers from the Baroque period. A further study of one of the most widely used band contest music lists, *The Interscholastic League Prescribed Music List,* from the state of Texas, reveals a substantial listing of these same works. The fact that such a large volume of music from this period has been published for band, espeically that of Bach and Handel, is indicative of the successful application of their music to wind and percussion instruments. This fact further indicates the popularity of the music of this period with school musicians and directors of our time. There is a valid reason for this popularity which is worthy of some discussion.

Both Bach and Handel produced a large number of compositions in a wide variety of forms in use during their time. These forms remain valid and popular today and include the chorale, the concerto, the prelude and fugue, as well as many of the short dance forms in both slow and fast tempos, including duple and triple meter. The length, difficulty, and authenticity of these original forms transcribe appropriately for both teaching and performing purposes of bands in the public schools.

Many of the works were transcribed from the original medium of organ, wind instruments, and voice, all of which adapt well to the wind band. In a few select instances, the compositions were originally scored for winds, such as the *Water Music* and the *Royal Fireworks Music* of Handel.

Both Bach and Handel scored in the full range of traditional harmonies, having at their disposal the organ as well as the orchestra. The band makes it possible to reproduce not only the polyphony, but the doubling in all registers of the woodwind and brass choirs for a valid and authentic transcription of the original work.

Many of the pieces are in the easier classifications of difficulty; grades I, II, and III. The rhythms are uncomplicated and the time signatures are traditional. The melodic content is pleasing and easy to comprehend for the young musician. The prelude and fugue form of Bach is challenging but comprehendable. His chorales have become an essential staple in the training repertoire of most bands regardless of maturity level.

A Style with Practical Application

In addition to all of the other advantages which make music of this period attractive to bands, it is probably the element of style which is most appealing to wind instrument players. The director who wishes to teach and emphasize the importance of note length and weight will find Baroque music most helpful. The music written for the Baroque organ was frequently bombastic and powerful. Wind players with expert guidance can emulate this style and improve upon the finesse and control over the medium for which the music was originally scored.

The melodies of that day which were produced by the somewhat monotonous mechanics of the organ are considerably enhanced by the delicate and subtle interpretation possible from a wind instrument player. The purity of timbre in the original settings for voice can, in the wind band, be duplicated in the separate woodwind and brass choirs, or enhanced and vitalized in combinations of woodwind and brass. In general, the band is able to duplicate most of the advantageous characteristics of the organ and human voice, and can often refine and improve the limited mechanical reproductive devices of that time.

The emulation of actual note length and weight is a skill which must begin within the first year of instrumental class instruction. The basic requirements of first-year objectives will safely accommodate the production of note lengths of (1) normally articulated duration; (2) separated, and consequently shorter duration; and (3) slurred, and consequently, maximum duration. The illustration for notation of such a teaching objective is shown in Figure 10-1.

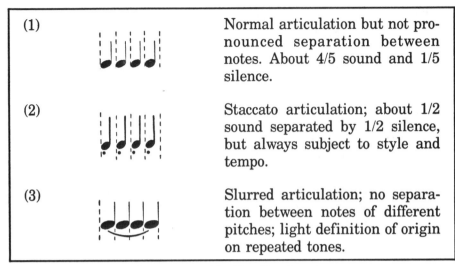

(1)		Normal articulation but not pronounced separation between notes. About 4/5 sound and 1/5 silence.
(2)		Staccato articulation; about 1/2 sound separated by 1/2 silence, but always subject to style and tempo.
(3)		Slurred articulation; no separation between notes of different pitches; light definition of origin on repeated tones.

Figure 10–1. First-Year Note Lengths.

The next logical extension in the control and definition of note length should be taught not later than the second year of instruction. This extension will include the difference between staccato and marcato weight, and the addition of legato. This knowledge expands the repertoire of articulation for the definition of musical style from three to five distinct lengths. (See Figure 10-2.) Most students can successfully interpret any music they are likely to encounter during their public school playing career with these skills in articulation.

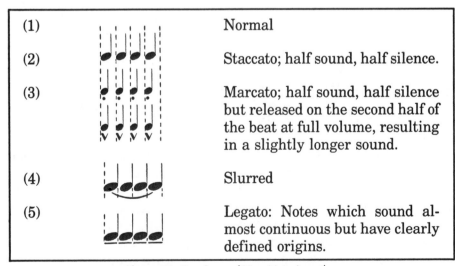

(1)		Normal
(2)		Staccato; half sound, half silence.
(3)		Marcato; half sound, half silence but released on the second half of the beat at full volume, resulting in a slightly longer sound.
(4)		Slurred
(5)		Legato: Notes which sound almost continuous but have clearly defined origins.

Figure 10–2 Second-Year Note Lengths.

The Advantages of Limited Dynamics and Tempos.

The fact that much of the music of the Baroque period was written for terrace dynamic levels is a controlling factor which immensely simplifies the musical demands on the wind player. Because of the limits of the organ and keyboard instruments of this period, there was seldom more than two dynamic levels required in a performance, and the need for the romantic crescendo did not exist. This music, then, becomes the ideal vehicle for training and reinforcing basic habits of articulation, separation, and connections of notes for wind players. The rubato in music of this period was unheard of; tempos were strict and even ritards were used sparingly. The band is afforded the opportunity to concentrate on consistency of a limited number of fundamentals in both note length and strength. Accents and explosive effects are not required. Dynamics are limited and generally apply to complete melodic phrases and sections which are often repeated in the same form at the second "terrace" level, thereby giving the student the opportunity to concentrate on dynamic changes without introducing new technical or melodic material.

Relating Problems of Tone Production to Baroque Style

The problems encountered by wind players in developing control of articulation and tone production of varying weight must be carefully monitored by the director. The implication in teaching becomes twofold: (1) the director must have a clear mental or aural image of correct style for the performance of music from each different period, and (2) the director must relate the mechanics of tone production and articulation to that which will have practical and musical application in later performance.

Wind players are much more likely to experience problems when required to produce short, rather than long, sounds. Here are some criteria for governing the minimum length of short sounds.

1. The length of the sound must not dictate an unusual articulation. Short notes must not suddenly become explosive attacks unless indicated by the composer.

2. The sound must be long enough to clearly identify the pitch notated.

3. The sound must have the characteristic quality of the instrument on which it is produced.

4. The sound must not deviate from the authentic or traditional length so much that it is uncharacteristic of the style.

Articulation Marks

The many interpretive score marks which are intended to define note length and strength are frequently a source of frustration to band directors. One must recognize the limits of the meaning of these marks and the lack of agreement between composers and arrangers in their application. This confusion applies to horizontal accents (>), vertical accents (∧), dots (•), lines (-), slurs (⌢), phrase marks (⌢⌣), and all conceivable combinations of these marks. A very complete discussion of this problem of application and interpretation is presented by W. Francis McBeth in his book *Effective Performance of Band Music.*

The following basic guidelines for the application of interpretive marks will be helpful. As the director gains experience in teaching and hearing correct style and correctly produced sound, it will make the application of these marks less confusing.

1. *Horizontal Accent* (>). This mark indicates emphasis by attack without distortion, achieved by increasing the force of the breath and the naturally increased action of the tongue. This action, in effect, produces the sound at a stronger dynamic level. The mark sometimes calls for notes of shorter duration, such as successive quarter notes in a march. In other applications it is important *not* to shorten the note. Such a case would be quarter triplets in traditional jazz scoring. At softer dynamic levels the mark can indicate emphasis on selected notes by simply separating and spacing without either increased attack or dynamic level.

2. *Vertical Accent (∧).* This accent usually indicates the strongest kind of emphasis employing forceful articulation, increased breath intensity, and a shorter note duration resulting in a louder sound and a separated style sometimes described as "marcato." Often a dot (•) or a line (-) is added to indicate less or more note length.

3. *Dot (•).* This mark is usually meant to indicate a short sound in staccato style. It must also be interpreted as a lighter attack, a necessary characteristic frequently overlooked. The rule for staccato is to shorten the note value by one-half of the original. The tempo and character of the music are determining factors in the ultimate length of notes thus marked, but a lightly articulated attack is imperative.

4. *Slur* (⌒). A curved line over two or more notes indicates that no articulation is to be used. This lack of articulation obviously becomes a different problem for trombone players who must then employ a connected legato articulation in combination with the use of natural slurs. The slur is frequently used in combination with dots (♪♪♪), or lines (♪♪♪)

to indicate a degree of decreased or increased articulation.

5. *Phrase* (⌒). A "phrase" is a longer line placed over a series of notes and/or measures intended to be played in a single breath and with a sense of musical continuity. The phrase mark is frequently misapplied by music editors and it can be confused with the slur; it is sometimes applied in easier band literature for the convenience of young performers instead of for musical effect, resulting in phrases which are fragmented by frequent breathing breaks.

In all matters of interpretation, musical judgment becomes a critical factor. A director should be encouraged to question certain features of the musical score. The interpretive markings discussed are certainly in that category. *The final decision must be based on what ultimately preserves the intent of the composer and the musical integrity of the piece.*

The Classical Period
The Music of Haydn and Mozart

The Classical period in music covered the years 1750 to 1820. This period began with the opera works of Gluck and the influence of Stamitz in the Mannheim orchestra. Other composers of the period included Catel, Jadin, and Gossec. Again, there emerged two towering musical figures who dominated the musical scene to the extent that the Classical period is also referred to as the "Age of Haydn and Mozart." The music of these two men was characterized by their adherence to perfection of form and meticulous order, and much of what they wrote was tailored for the orchestra which was undergoing a period of reform and refinement. The strings were being provided four true parts of independent importance, the reeds were much improved, and the clarinet was accepted for the first time into a true role in the woodwind section. The brass winds continued to function as inflexible open-tone instruments, contributing largely to the dynamic reinforcement of the larger ensemble. Independence for the brass family was being delayed for the mechanical development of the valved instruments. The use of percussion was limited to prevent its encroachment into the light and lyric style which the composers demanded and prescribed for the orchestra. It is almost predictable that music composed in such a structured environment would not transcribe as easily into the repertoire of the band. As a result, the works of the composers of this period are not as widely performed by bands. Even the works of Beethoven, which were beginning a transition toward Romanticism, fail to find practical application in the literature of the wind band.

Some Problems in Classical Music for Bands

Band transcriptions and arrangements of the Classical period are not as numerous as those of either the Baroque or Romantic period, but the compositions of Haydn and Mozart easily dominate the listing found in *Band Music Guide*. The Classical works have also been steadily deleted from the *University Interscholastic Prescribed Music* lists. This author's personal experience in contest and festival adjudication supports the infrequency with which these composers are played for such occasions.

It is not too difficult to understand the reason why Classical music has not gained favor with the band medium. The principal characteristics of this music are simplicity, transparency, and lightness, all conceived for a limited wind and percussion section. Most of the melodic and rhythmic activity takes place in the violin section of the orchestral works. Percussion is usually limited to the tympani, using only two kettles. One who would transcribe such a work for band is faced with the need for a rather complete and skilled woodwind choir for the bulk of such writing. The brass choir is often relegated to the task of counting long periods of rest only to add four quarter notes at the end of the final phase.

There are some excellent Classical compositions which bands will continue to perform. The most popular composer is probably Mozart; his works often find favor with the band that has developed a good clarinet section, and who wish to explore and expand their technical facility. This feature coupled with a band that is experiencing a weak brass section (which should attempt nothing more difficult than counting rests and finalizing phrases) often makes such a selection ideal. Some selections by Mozart which are often heard include:

1. *The Impressario,* arr. Barnes,...Published by Ludwig Music Pub. Co.

2. *Marriage of Figaro,* arr. Duthoit,...Published by Boosey Hawkes

These compositions have somewhat similar requirements in achieving the correct style. The first and most important objective is to understand and achieve a correct staccato style. The initial reaction to such efforts is almost universally a forcefully articulated attack in an effort to produce a short note. It has been pointed out previously that this effort is absolutely the wrong response required of the staccato style. It is important to again be reminded that the textbook definition of staccato says nothing about "emphasis"; rather, it would be well to think in terms of "de-emphasis" for those players who want to achieve the characteristic lightness required in this style.

Technical Problems in the Performance of Mozart

The woodwind choir, in the performance of Mozart, will frequently be required to articulate four notes on a beat at a fairly rapid (108 mm or more) tempo. These passages should not be considered to require staccato tonguing such as that applied to quarter notes in the same tempo. If the original reference to note length in staccato style is used, there is hardly a need to shorten eighth notes to one-half their original value when grouped in fours and moving rapidly in succession. The best possible advice for clarinet players under such conditions is to apply the absolute opposite technique by using a "dah" articulation normally reserved for legato playing. This serves to remove the possibility of explosiveness from the attacks and keeps the tongue as close as possible to the reed. By decreasing the distance it must travel, the effect is to improve the tongue speed. The patient application of this technique will produce good results as the passage begins to approach the performance tempo. The ease and relaxation which becomes a part of the playing will be a small compromise to note length in exchange for a vastly more musical performance.

Another approach to staccato playing is sure to sound inconsistent at first, but will solve yet another major traditional problem in performing music in the Classical style. This approach has even a more universal application to other wind literature. The problem is the performance (especially in Haydn and Mozart) of punctuational chords at the end of phrases and on strong beats of the measure within the phrase that are often scored for brass or woodwind choirs independently, and then, at some point, for the entire band. The difficulty is often heightened by a compassionate transcriber who chooses to ignore the original score and write dynamically reinforcing parts for snare drum, bass drum, and cymbals.

Interpretation of Other Short Sounds

The scoring of chordal accompaniment for emphasis and punctuation usually appears as quarter notes, keeping within the style and tempo of the piece. The usual sequence for such scoring would be for accompaniment during the phrase, and at the phrase ending or cadence. A variety of minor variations on secondary or offbeats can be included in this category. The most important concern about such scoring is that the composer has chosen to reinforce the tonality with a chord, much as the pianist might choose to play a four-note chord with both hands on the keyboard. Occasionally such reinforcement is scored in unison or at the octave. This scoring must also be dealt with in a manner similar to that of harmonic scoring. The director's first responsibility, in this case, is to identify and balance the chord at an appropriate dynamic level. It is frequently helpful to ask the ensemble to sustain the note to gain a better perspective of the composer's intent. The principle of the pyramid balance is completely applicable in this instance, with the bottom or tonic sound being as much as two-thirds stronger than the very top note in the instrumentation. The second requirement is for the director to establish the proper length of each sound in the pattern.

In a large majority of cases in practice, the quarter notes are played too short. A zealous music editor or arranger often complicates the matter by adding staccato dots over the notes [musical notation] or various accents [musical notation]. The culminating assurance for a musical abortion comes with the addition of an "f" or "ff" dynamic marking to match that which applies to the rest of the ensemble. Suddenly the opportunity for musical disaster has become legion. The inexperienced player takes all of the advice written on the music, acknowledges the encouragement of an inexperienced conductor who flails the air with heavy accents at the forte level, and bursts forth with clipped and percussive attacks which completely destroy the ensemble quality of the entire band. This is often aided and abetted by a snare drummer (or two or three) who have been saving their energies, and at long last have an opportunity to play a few notes with all of the vitality required for a two hundred-piece marching band.

It is important to note here that everyone in the foregoing scenario did exactly what the instructive markings on the score told them to do. Such a condition obviously signals the need for some kind of musical detective to assemble a set of musical clues which permit an accurate portrayal of correct musical style. Here are a few key remedies suggested to arrest or prevent such a musical disaster from developing.

1. A rule having widespread application is: Notes surrounded by rests should be played full value. This would apply also to notes preceded by rests or followed by rests, including phrases beginning with pickups as well as phrase endings. It seems logical that the composer, by isolating the sounded note in a span of silence (the rests), has indicated his true feeling about the length of sound desired. To further interpret such notes with the addition of a staccato mark or articulation is contrary to the principle of sound production of the wind instruments. The sound produced by a wind instrument decays almost immediately upon termination of its energy source or air supply. The problem arises when we fail to understand this important mechanic of transcribing the part from a string to a wind instrument. The resonating string continues to sound after it is bowed or plucked, producing a sonority which the classical composer used as a compositional tool of expression. The marks and rhythms were entirely appropriate for the orchestral strings, but they do not translate literally to the band.

2. The practice of using a common dynamic level for an entire ensemble, including both primary melodic and accompaniment material, originated with the orchestra. As such, the numerical proportion of strings to winds is quite different from the proportion of the clarinet choir (functioning as the string section) and the remainder of the band including the large percussion ensemble. There is no conceivable way that such dynamic markings can produce results emulating the traditional sound of the period of Classicism.

A thoughtful study of the score of any transcription will reveal numerous problem areas which can be anticipated by the director. Such techniques can be defined and effectively digested by the student musicians so that they make musically mature judgments for an effective musical performance.

The Romantic Period

The Age of Wagner

The Romantic period in music history extended from 1820 to 1900. The popular composers of that period are numerous, including Berlioz, Liszt, Brahms, Verdi, Saint-Saens, Mendelssohn, Bizet, Massenet, Rimsky-Korsakov, Tchaikovsky, Bruckner, Mahler, and Strauss. The National school of the period included Elgar, Grieg, Smetana, Dvorak, Chopin, and Franck. The list can be expanded with many more names who made substantial contributions, but the name of Richard Wagner perhaps best characterizes the musical impact of the Romantic era. These European composers amassed a storehouse of music which has provided the band with much transcribed and transcribable literature. The emergence of credible performing units in colleges and universities in the late 1930's stimulated the desire for worthy music. Skilled American band conductors such as Austin Harding, the Goldmans, and Mark Hindsley began to arrange compositions of the great Classical and Romantic periods which formed the basis of a solid core of band literature. These creative efforts continued through the years to provide quality music for bands.

In recent years the music of Wagner and his contemporaries has appeared less frequently on the required music lists across the country. This absence reflects several conditions, none of which diminish the quality or usefulness of Romantic music for bands. Probably the most valid reason that less of this music is included on published lists is that an entirely new store of literature has come into existence from current band composers. These new compositions represent the beginnings of the band's own library which has long been a serious concern. Band conductors of the past twenty years seem eager to embrace these new works as an important element of the band's development into the world of serious performing mediums. A second condition might be that the major works of Wagner, Berlioz, Tchaikovsky, and others are among the more difficult grades of band literature and their effective performance is restricted to better high school and college bands. There seems to be less Romantic literature transcribed for band in Grades I, II, and III than, for example, the compositions of Bach and Handel. Another condition which tends to limit the use of these transcriptions is the increased emphasis on the percussion ensemble in today's organizations. Those bands that chose to dedicate large amounts of rehearsal time in preparation of a major work prefer to be able to challenge all sections of the band instead of only the winds, as is the case with most transcribed literature.

Despite the difficulties in playing music of the Romantic Period, adjudicators across the country continue to hear the great Wagner, Strauss, Tchaikovsky, and Mahler works in contest performances where there are no restrictions on the selection of program. Generally, more mature bands choose to address these pieces because of their technical demands and the increased importance of overall interpretive problems.

The Romantic Style

When compared to Baroque and Classical composition, the distinguishing characteristic revealed in Romantic music is its overall complexity. Instead of readily identifiable phrases and themes, the conductor is presented with melodic ideas which last for many measures. Such melodies must be nurtured patiently and meticulously to achieve the musical effect of climax intended by the composer. The dynamic markings include every conceivable level and shading over long periods of development with punctuating and explosive indications seldom required before. The structure of tonality and chromaticism of Wagner requires an unlimited level of ability from the individual musician who must fit the individual lines into keys which pass as frequently as the beats in a given measure.

The expanded form that came into use during this period requires musical maturity of both player and conductor which assumes a complete technical competence. The musical demands of tempi and rubato cannot be inhibited by a student still struggling with the mechanics of the instrument. The musically conceptual skill of the conductor must have an unlimited horizon for transmitting a mature emotional experience to the performing ensemble. The conductor's obligations of controlling the complex lines, textures, and harmonies in Romantic music present a formidable task.

Conceptions and Misconceptions of Interpretation

The performance of Romantic music is frequently misunderstood. The complexity described in this music is not in the number or velocity of notes written into the parts. Tragically humorous stories abound about directors who choose the *Trauersinfonie* of Richard Wagner as a warm-up march because the time signature is in cut time. Even the hundreds of conductors who basically understand the notation of this work are seldom able to transmit the musical importance of the notes to their band. All too often Romantic pieces, including even works like *Prelude and Love Death* from "Tristan and Isolde," are chosen for performance because "the notes aren't hard."

In summary, here are some of the challenges one must be prepared to meet when moving from the Baroque and Classical periods to the Romantic period.

1. Instead of short phrases and musical ideas, one is faced with lengthy and expanded melodies and phrases.

2. Instead of terrace or two and three dynamic levels, there are at least six distinct levels ranging from ppp to fff.

3. Instead of strict predictable tempos, you have constantly changing rubato effects, long accelerandos, and ritards with demanding accompanying dynamic levels.

4. Instead of predictable key relationships, there is a constant mobility of key and chromatic activity.

5. Instead of simple structure and balance problems within the ensemble, one is faced with tonal effects that require absolute individual authenticity in characteristic sound with enormous physical demands in phrase length.

6. Instead of clear and basic demands of note length and weight, there is a great variety of emphasis on individual tones which test the skill and ability of every wind player.

7. Instead of light and delicate quality, there are rich, heavy and sonorous individual and ensemble sounds.

Some pieces which still often appear on various required music lists include:

Berlioz:	*Beatrice and Benedict Overture,* Arr. Henning...Published by Carl Fischer.

Mendelssohn:	*Overture for Band,* Arr. Greissle... Published by Schirmer *Fingal's Cave,* Arr. Winterbottom... Published by Boosey Hawkes
Rimsky-Korsakov:	*Cappricio Espanol,* Arr. Winterbottom... Published by Boosey Hawkes.
Tchaikovsky:	*Finale, Symphony No. 4,* Arr. Safranek... Published by Carl Fischer.
Wagner:	*Prelude and Love Death* (From "Tristan and Isolde") Arr. Godfrey... Published by Boosey Hawkes. *Liebestod,* Arr. Bainum...Published by Kjos Music Co. *Siegfried's Rhine Journey,* Arr. Cailliet... Published by Carl Fischer. *Elsa's Procession to the Cathedral,* Arr. Cailliet...Published by Remick. *Trauersinfonie,* Arr. Leidzen...Published by Ludwig. *Album Leaf,* Arr. Johnson...Published by Rubank.
Mahler:	*First Movement: Symphony No. 3,* Arr. Schaefer...Published by TRN.

The Contemporary Period

Classical and Romantic Techniques in Modern Band Music

The "modern" or contemporary period of classical and romantic music is something which may well be unique to the band music field. The style of this music utilizes many of the techniques in scoring and interpretation which is common in its historical predecessors. A rather broad separation of two groups of composers under this heading would include those within the 1900 to 1950 era, and those producing largely band compositions since 1950. The pre-1950 group would include Hanson, Strauss, Holst, Bartok, Vaughan Williams, Shostakovich, Hindemith, Ravel, Gershwin, and Grainger, to name but a few. This particular group is further classified into various school of "isms" such as Neoromanticism, Nationalism, Impressionism, etc. While many of these composers arrived at the band through various other mediums, some such as Holst and Grainger, gave the band a first ray of hope for its *own* identity and literature.

Since 1950, a dramatic acceleration in the development of the symphonic band resulted from an almost natural alliance forged with the contemporary composers of this period. As the desire for new band literature began too increase, the prospect of performance and financial rewards for the composer became a reality. It became possible for a composer of band music to become a full-time professional, and many competent (and some incompetent) musicians began pouring their talents and energies into writing for this medium.

It has been an interesting phenomenon to witness the vigor and enthusiasm with which wind band players and conductors embrace the availability of new band literature. With the exception of a few professional military service bands, this movement is seated in the public schools and universities of our country. It should be observed that these teaching skills, which promote the performance of this endless flow of literature, are sustained at the grass-roots level by hundreds of marvelously skilled and intensely motivated young band conductors in the public schools.

It is no secret that the traditional world of artistic media has chosen not to "legitimatize" the band music composer with an appropriate place in music history, but this is not entirely without cause. Considering how long it took even band conductors to pass from a state of disdain to understanding band works like *Lincolnshire Posey* and the *Hindemith Symphony in B♭*, it is small wonder that musical acceptance in the "nonband" world is slow to come. The evolution of band literature may well make for itself a place of its own. The original role of the band as a functional rather than a musical ensemble—first in military service and later in athletic service—is a matter of record. Some would commit an unpardonable error of denying this ancestry in a synthetic effort to elevate the band's birthright to something "more worthy of the arts." However, this false elevation will not come to pass, and bands will remain rooted to their origins, which is not to deny their rise to a rightful place in music history.

The interpretation of modern band music will have a major impact upon the acceptance of this new source of literature. Admittedly, not all of the music which has been and will be published is worthy, but it must be given a fair hearing. There is a vast challenge for the young conductor to understand and interpret new band literature. Without a background in teaching and conducting even traditional literature, modern band music with the addition of asymmetric rhythms and atonality seems almost like a foreign tongue in music. Fortunately, the solution to the problem is not as complex as it may seem.

Classifying Modern Band Composers

Francis McBeth divides the works of prominent band composers into broad categories of the "classicist" and the "romanticist." The interpretation and the preparation of the performance of these composers' works relates directly to the same techniques used in music of "The" Romantic and "The" Classical periods. It is extremely helpful to examine McBeth's grouping of band composers in the categories following:*

*These lists have been expanded by the author.

Primarily Romanticists:

Hanson, Howard (use for a model)

Arnold, Malcolm

Bassett, Leslie

Chance, John Barnes

Creston, Paul

Finney, Charles

Giannini, Vittorio

Grainger, Percy

Hindemith, Paul

Husa, Karel

Jenkins, Joseph Willcox

McBeth, Francis

Primarily Classicists:

Persichetti, Vincent (use for a model)

Carter, Charles

Copeland, Aaron

Hartley, Walter

Jacob, Gordon

Kirk, Theron

Latham, William (late works romantic)

White, Donald

Varying Degree—Classical and Romantic:

Bennett, Robert Russell

Primarily Romanticists:	Varying Degree—Classical and Romantic:
Mennin, Peter	Dahl, Ingolf
Nelhybel, Vaclav	Dello Joio, Norman
Nixon, Roger	Giovannini, Caesar
Orff, Carl	Gould, Morton
Penderecki, Krzysztof	Grundman, Clare
Reed, Alfred	Holst, Gustav
Reed, H. Owen	Jager, Robert
Schoenberg, Arnold	Whear, Paul
Smith, Claude	
Tull, Fisher	
Vaughan Williams, Ralph	
Williams, Clifton	

An examination of the music of these composers and a comparison of compositional techniques within and between categories should help the band conductor in the performance of these works.

The Music of Percy Grainger

One of the most typical romanticists was Percy Aldridge Grainger. His understanding and, at the same time, *lack* of understanding of the wind band, produced some of the most imaginative music in all of band literature. His unfamiliarity with the limits of the winds and percussion, and at the same time disdain for traditional limitations, provided the basis for a new freedom in band writing. Grainger's early experiences as a saxophonist in the British army bands seems to have provided an impetus for band composing, which when formalized through the wisdom of a concert pianist, produced a revelation in sound for wind and percussion instruments. The pioneer independence which prompted him to hike miles between concert appearances seemed also to free his musical genius from any and all restrictions of notation and meter in *Lincolnshire Posey.* Yet, almost every composition attributed to Grainger today was a "setting" of a traditional melody or folksong and falls almost perfectly into the pattern of emotional (Wagnerian, if you will) romanticism.

And so the common bond of emotional response through melody, development, and effects can be traced through the works of Howard Hanson, Francis McBeth, Alfred Reed, Karel Husa, and all of the others. Once the conductor can identify and accept the characteristics of either the modern classical or romantic composer, the process of correct interpretation may begin to develop. It is important at this point to understand the common denominator between modern band compositions and traditional music of that time.

Applying Traditional Concepts to Band Music

As a word of caution, one should not become confused or misdirected by the introduction of contemporary tonality, unusual orchestration, or complex rhythms and meter. These elements generally do not change the interpretation of basic style in music. It is quite common for the inexperienced or unskilled conductor of bands to become completely ineffective with a composition by Hindemith, Husa, or even Persichetti. The cause is almost universally an inability to hear tonality. The problems of complex scoring and rhythm frequently add to the conductor's confusion. The similarity of style is often completely overlooked such as the likeness between a traditional Bach chorale and "So Pure the Star" by Perischetti. These compositions have much the same requirements of phrasing and structure in the wind band, but often the conductor is unable to identify the common elements of voice leading, harmonic structure, and chord progressions which can be treated similarly.

Performance standards for modern band literature must be based on the same elements of music expression listed at the beginning of this chapter:

1. Correct style, rhythm, tempo, and note length and weight
2. Correct dynamic levels
3. Control of phrasing in conveying musical ideas

These elements are separate from the requirements of: blend, balance, tone quality, and intonation. In summary, it may again be pointed out that a performance can have each of these qualities without achieving the status of a convincing musical experience. Perfect intonation, absolute control of balance, and well-blended sound are only parts of the goal of ensemble performance. These features are often expected and achieved by amateur groups, but true maturity in performance must go beyond to include the elements of music.

BIBLIOGRAPHY

American School Band Directors Association, Donald W. McCabe, Project Chairperson. *The ASBOA Curriculum Guide* (Pittsburgh, PA: Volkwein Brothers, Inc., 1973)

Fennell, Frederick. "Basic Band Repertory: British Band Classics from the Conductor's Point of View," *The Instrumentalist,* (1980).

Goldman, Richard Franko. *The Wind Band and Its Literature.* (Boston, MA: Allyn and Bacon, 1967)

Green, Elizabeth A. H., and Nicolai Malko. *The Conductor and His Score.* (Englewood Cliffs, NJ: Prentice-Hall, Inc., 1975)

Labuta, Joseph A. *Teaching Musicianship in the High School Band.* (West Nyack, NY: Parker Publishing Company, Inc., 1972)

Linton, Stanley. *Conducting Fundamentals.* (Englewood Cliffs, NJ: Prentice-Hall, Inc., 1982)

Prausnitz, Frederik. *Score and Podium.* (New York, NY: W. W. Norton and Company, Inc., 1983)

Westrup, J. A., and F. L. Harrison. *The New College Encyclopedia of Music.* (New York, NY: W. W. Norton and Company, revised 1976)

Willoughby, David. *Comprehensive Musicianship and Undergraduate Music Curricula.* (Reston, VA: MENC Publications, Sales Center for Educational Associations, 1971)

11

Evaluating Performance

Over a period of many years during which the author has participated in, conducted, and adjudicated band performances, the strengths and weaknesses of these performances seem to have a characteristic pattern. The strength of bands can be summarized by stating that the level of bands in the public schools has improved dramatically. This improvement is the direct result of:

1. Better-funded support for the band program within the curriculum of the schools and for salaries
2. Improved teacher training programs in colleges and universities
3. A steady flow of band literature for all levels of advancement
4. Constantly expanded opportunities for performance exposure, including athletic and community service, and contest and festival events

While all four factors have contributed to better bands, the element of contest and festival competition has brought about the recognition of outstanding examples of not only technically proficient, but also stirring musical performances in which each of the elements discussed in Chapter 10 are presented and mastered in a professional manner.

FACTORS THAT INFLUENCE PERFORMANCES

It is not too difficult to isolate certain characteristic flaws that cause bands to fail to achieve satisfactory performance standards. These shortcomings fall into the two categories of (a) technical and mechanical elements, and (b) musical elements. It is easy to lapse into conjecture about which of these two comes first (much like the chicken or the egg theory), but since technical weaknesses are more easily identified, they will be described first. It is also true that the sequence of instruction in the natural development of the player stresses certain technical skills before the process of making music can actually take place.

Common Technical Flaws

Immature and Uncharacteristic Sound

The lack of characteristic tone quality is a common trait in a band performance which does not qualify for a top evaluative rating. It is even more detrimental to solo and ensemble performance where isolation of the instruments make the flaw so much more obvious. Immature and uncharacteristic sound in the woodwind choir seems to detract more from an effective performance than in the brass choir or percussion ensemble. Poor quality in the flute, clarinet, and saxophone sections contributes to more low contest ratings than any other major factor. Band conductors and teachers need to recognize the unique problems of achieving correct sound from this critical group of instruments. Clarinet players, for example, simply do not develop the same degree of maturity in tone quality as most members of the brass choir receiving an equal amount of training. Trumpet students more often achieve a natural sound without special help while members of the woodwind family almost never do so without special attention.

Problems of the Flute and Clarinet

The defects of tone on clarinet and flute are manifested in a number of ways. Overblowing the instrument in the upper register without accompanying support is probably the most common. Almost as frequent is the habit of propelling too little air through the instrument, thereby producing a wheezy sound on clarinet and a whistling tone on flute. Such sounds have neither a tunable pitch center nor a tonal center. The latter condition of underplaying often comes about as a result of a conductor who has been criticized for letting clarinets and flutes play too loudly with an accompanying thin quality. The conductor accordingly reduces the volume of the problem by making the players blow softer without ever addressing the real source of the problem. This "sotta voce" approach is certainly less offensive than the shrill treble quality produced by the section which overblows and undersupports, but the real problem is still present.

The Clarinet Embouchure

Much of the difficulty for woodwinds originates with a failure to understand how to form the correct embouchure. Unlike producing a sound on a brass instrument where the lips have natural support to begin vibration on the mouthpiece, the clarinet player must control a variety of muscles around the vibrating source, some of which pull toward the mouthpiece and reed, and others which pull away to flatten the chin surface. Even when the director correctly identifies the problem and knows the solution, there seems to be a lack of ability to convey its importance in motivating the student to correct the deficiency. It seems clear that neither the conductor nor the players fully appreciate the detrimental effect on a musical performance.

Improper Breathing

Improper breathing and use of the breath in providing support for correct sound is a common flaw in many wind groups. Here again, it causes woodwinds to sound more immature than brass players of equal experience. The nature of tone production on a brass instrument normally demands more air pressure and encourages somewhat better breathing habits than for woodwinds. This fact, however, does not assure proper use of the air in the all-important matter of breath support for correct tone production.

French Horn Tone Quality

The matter of correct tone quality on French horn, as in all brasses, relates to embouchure tension and the correct use of the breath. The additional factor of hand placement in the bell of the horn seems to be a complicating feature uncommon to the other instruments. Added to that is the difficulty of tonal control in various partials of the playing register which are more flexible than on other brass instruments. French horn sound is seldom harmful to the ensemble because it is too loud. Rather, the deficiency results from a lack of good horn sound to support the critical middle register of the band sonority.

Hiding Flaws in Controlled Dynamics

A great many bands maintain their best ensemble sound at a dynamic level between mezzo piano and mezzo forte. There are several reasons for this. These are levels which require less energy and are "convenient" for the student. A daily routine of rehearsal which has few demands for real effort toward improvement from the conductor permits a student to acquire a habit of playing at this level. There is little emphasis in rehearsing controlled sound at dynamic extremes. This produces bands in performance who are unable to control a genuine forte or piano dynamic level without losing the characteristic sound.

A second flaw which develops from the same basic problem causes poorly blended and balanced ensemble or section quality. The more mature players on top parts play with a wider range of dynamics while others stay in the same narrow range of a convenient level. Trumpets, first clarinets, and flutes crescendo to a "ff" easily while tuba, horn, bass clarinet, and third clarinet players make considerably smaller variations in color and quality with a resulting emphasis on treble voices as the group approaches the apex of the crescendo.

Problems in Percussion

The percussion ensemble is frequently at fault in matters that relate to the production of proper tone quality. Instruments in this area that most often need correction are the cymbals, bass drum, and tympani. A great majority of percussionists have not been trained to evaluate the need for either quality or quantity of sound in relation to the total ensemble effect. Cymbal players are most notorious for producing crash effects that interrupt and frequently destroy that portion of a band performance. Without getting into all of the wrong ways to play this instrument, the conductor could greatly benefit the performance by simply assessing the amount of sound needed for the size of the wind group at a characteristic dynamic level. Many students are completely unaware that their efforts can easily produce a cymbal crash appropriate for a 200-piece band. With proper advice from the podium, this sound can be scaled down to the needs of a 40-, 50-, or 60-piece band.

The bass drummer frequently has similar problems in the production of an appropriate volume of sound. The techniques of stroke, head position, and damping are a bit more complicated on this instrument. These deficiencies can be masked to some extent by simply coaching the player to react with some restraint, and at appropriate varying dynamic levels. The bass drummer who beats the head incessantly throughout an entire march at the same fortissimo level of the introduction is all too common.

The problem of the snare drum sound in most bands is simply a matter of proper head and snare tension. The heads should generally be tight enough to produce a relatively high-pitched sound. The snare should also be taut. This combination will produce a crisp sound with a minimum of roar and reverberation which might otherwise interfere with the wind sonority.

Tympani players, with the addition of various pitches at their disposal, have more ways in which to depreciate a band performance. In addition to playing too loudly, the tympanist can also play each and every note anywhere from fractionally off-pitch to several interval steps away from correct pitch. Again, without discussing basic playing techniques, it is easy for the conductor to diagnose a possible problem of volume when the player originates the stroke from the shoulder at a height of more than twelve inches from the kettle. Proper tone production in completely sufficient amounts can be produced without such hammering blows to the drum. Still, the more harmful effect of playing wrong or improperly tuned notes during a performance is the more common flaw in tympani playing.

The frustration of listening to a student search for the correct tuning note on the tympani just before a contest performance is all too familiar to those who have judged such events. On such occasions the student moves the pedal up and down, never once approaching the correct tone, and finally with the full approval of the conductor, leaves it set at random to begin the performance.

Problems of Tone Quality Induced by Articulation

Improper employment of the tongue in starting and articulating tones is yet another common problem in performance. It is a continuation of the problem of the mismanagement of the correct use of the breath.

The most detrimental articulated effect occurs in staccato playing. Misuse and misinterpretation of this articulation mark by editors, composers, and transcribers have served to compound the problem. Assuming that the application of the staccato dot over or under the note is intended to shorten the original value, the common problem for wind players is to do so without increasing the actual force or volume of the tone. A universal and natural reaction in producing shorter sounds is to increase the speed of the air by releasing it with a harder stroke of the tongue. In addition to a shorter tone, we now also have an explosive beginning, the exact opposite of what is normally intended by the staccato marking.

In woodwinds and brass alike, the staccato problem relates to the basic mechanical skill of starting the tone. Clarinets or trumpets who have difficulty in starting a tone softly must, by habit, force more air into the instrument to make it respond.

Notes marked with either the horizontal or vertical accent are also frequently misinterpreted. The results are not quite as harmful since the accent normally requires a more forceful attack. The most common error is in application of the sforzando attack to such notes. As stated previously, these accents must be interpreted in the context of the nature and style of the music.

Faulty Tone Production that Produces Poor Intonation

Nearly everything that relates to use of the breath and formation of the correct embouchure in wind players affects correct intonation. The problems in performance are obvious: Trumpets play sharp when producing tones in the low register. Clarinets are often sharp when playing softly below the break and on throat tones. Students must be made to realize that every change in volume and register requires some compensating adjustment on each and every note. These adjustments must be made *during a performance* by minute muscular contraction and relaxation in the embouchure, fractional changes in air pressure from the diaphragm, and changes in direction of the air stream through movement of the head position. It is highly unlikely that such critical control of the entire physical and mechanical playing environment can occur until the student has acquired a reasonably correct embouchure, hand and instrument position, and breathing and support habits. An incorrectly produced sound is virtually inflexible. Such a sound is not mechanically centered and causes all of the pitches on the instrument to respond unpredictably. Under such conditions, tones which are traditionally good tuning notes will respond sharp or flat and lead to unusual tuning adjustments that, in turn, will intensify other tuning problems on the instrument.

Inability to Reach a Common Pitch Level

Some bands that achieve reasonably good individual tuning have difficulty in finding and adhering to a common pitch level within the band between sections and major choirs. In such cases the entire brass choir may be tuned well above the level of the woodwind choir. The reasons that such conditions develop are varied but the solution is relatively simple. Establishment of a tuning group to originate and set the pitch level as outlined in Chapter 9 is a first step. Continued reference to this group, by having them play a portion of a scale in initial adjustment of all instruments, is mandatory. It is quite easy for brasses in general to begin listening to the first trumpet for pitch adjustment during performance. At the same time, the woodwind choir begins to gravitate toward the level of the top clarinets. When these two levels are different a band can quite innocently arrive at two differing levels of tuning, either before or during an actual performance.

Some tuning practices which do not produce good results are: full band tuning by playing a scale in parallel thirds or fifths; tuning to the lowest voice in the band such as the tuba; and tuning to a pitch sounded by a mallet instrument such as marimba or xylophone. The scale in unison or octaves provides the best comparative-listening opportunity for tuning.

Mistakes in Rhythm and Interpretation of Note Values

The most common error in the performance of the standard march occurs in playing 6/8 rhythms. The usual tendency is to add time to the quarter note and subtract it from the eighth note when played in sequence. The effect is to convert the pattern into a 2/4 feeling. Occasionally the opposite problem occurs in 2/4 time by converting the dotted eighth-sixteenth pattern into one that sounds more like the 6/8 notation.

An absolute and correct performance of the traditional dotted eighth-sixteenth pattern is subject to some interpretation. In music of many Classical and Romantic composers, the common practice is to lengthen the dotted eighth and shorten the sixteenth note, leaning slightly in the direction of a 30-second note value. This practice is seldom criticized even in the performance of a modern march such as "Proud Heritage" by William Latham. The entire matter is not often questioned as long as the short note (16th) does not take on an explosive or accented feeling and the total effect continues the phrase line with good musical flow instead of interruption.

The compression or rushing of note values such as two eighth notes or four sixteenth notes in succession is a regular occurrence in many bands. The practice becomes emphasized by immature groups who are performing music beyond the limits of their technical ability. A notoriously abused and well-known transcription with this problem is the "Finale" to the Fourth Symphony of Tchaikovsky. The cascading groups of sixteenth notes passed from one section to another seldom fall into a smooth progressive line of equal sounds. Each group of four is compressed enough to leave a telltale gap before the next set of voices takes up the passage.

Strangely enough, even the less-complicated rhythms fall prey to this same malady. Only the very well-schooled groups seem to accurately convey rhythms like "quarter, eighth-eighth, quarter, eighth-eighth" without rushing the latter part of the measure. The possibilities for error in this area are endless and relate directly to the failure of the student to form a habit of subdividing each and every beat mentally. It has been the author's experience that those bands who have been exposed to the breath impulse method as beginners are substantially more accurate in such matters. Even bands which regularly vocalize standard rhythm counting in rehearsal will play with improved stability over other groups.

Failure to Achieve Ensemble Balance

Improper balance in band performance is normally easy to hear. The effect of poorly blended tone quality is more difficult to diagnose during a performance because it is easily confused with poor intonation and generally occurs in combination with it.

Bands which have balance problems in a performance frequently have a wide difference of maturity level within the group. The most common flaws include treble voices and percussion sections which play too loudly in proportion to the amount of sound being produced by the lower part of the brass and woodwind choirs. Such performances are dominated by the sound of top clarinet and trumpet, or occasionally by the flutes. Unfortunately, this condition is often accompanied by poor tone quality from the same dominating voices. An imbalance in proper instrumentation can also magnify the problem.

While not all of these balance problems can be easily resolved, most of them could be measurably alleviated by simply controlling the volume level of the offending instruments to put them into perspective of the pyramid concept of band structure. Even the bands which have no French horns, weak tubas, and weak trombones can help their condition by correctly structuring the saxophones and woodwind choir.

Balance Problems of the Traditional March

Bands which use older standard marches by King, Jewell, Chambers, etc. for the warm-up number immediately create a challenge in correct balance. Many of these selections base their major harmonic framework on the sounds scored for tuba and French horns. The pattern in marches by Karl King starts with a unison introduction followed by a first strain of melody in duet form, usually scored for flute, clarinet, and cornet. The band with limited instrumentation and immature players on lower parts is doomed from the start in attempting a quality performance. In selecting and rehearsing such a march, the conductor might start by designating all of the voices which play a harmony part, exclusive of the melodic ensemble. These voices would include tuba, baritone saxophone, bass clarinet, French horn, third trombone, and sometimes trombone and trumpet parts which are scored like the horns. If this particular group of intruments can achieve a satisfactory ensemble sound of good quality, it is safe to proceed with the addition of the melodic ensemble which will include perhaps two-thirds of the band. This larger group of remaining instruments must be judiciously controlled to keep from causing the balance problems which traditionally mar such a performance.

When assessing and diagnosing good balance within the total ensemble, it is always helpful to listen for the correct structure in the three basic ensembles which go to make up the symphonic band: percussion, brass, and woodwind. The separate voices and sections of each of these groups must retain a characteristic strength unless performing in a solo capacity.

Balance Problems During the Crescendo.

Finally, the problems in balance that originate when bands change dynamic levels are all too frequent. The circumstances that create this problem seem relatively simple to understand. As music requires volume changes either suddenly or gradually through crescendo, the strength of individuals and sections does not change equally or proportionately. Again, many conductors do not understand the pyramid principle of band structure which dictates substantially more effort from low voices within the ensemble. If each part in the brass choir plays twice as loud when progressing from piano to forte, the top voices (trumpets) will sound too loud in proportion to the tuba, baritone, trombone, and French horn parts. The art of changing dynamic levels without destroying balance requires a wider variation in effort from the lower voices in order to produce sounds of sufficient strength for correct balance.

This balance problem is further compounded in a band which has an incorrect ratio of voices in its instrumentation. The band with one tuba, one baritone, two trombones and two French horns in the same choir with nine trumpets has a natural problem. Considerable restraint must be imposed on the trumpet section to achieve a structured sound with any degree of acceptable balance. The woodwind choir with large numbers of soprano clarinets and flutes without bass and contra-bass clarinets must address the same problem.

Common Musical Flaws

The entire realm of creating a musically effective performance can be a perplexing challenge to the young conductor who may not have a natural sensitivity for this quality. Many books and articles have been written on the subject and a comprehensive treatment will not be attempted here. Yet there are certain fundamental characteristics of musicality in performance which can be rather easily identified and categorized. Application of corrective measures for the four rather common flaws described here are completely within reach of most all band conductors in the performance of the easier grades of band literature. The problems continue to surface and go uncorrected largely because they are overlooked in favor of more pressing priorities such as learning the music and correcting technical problems. The two elements of technical and musical preparation are quite easily combined with a proper awareness and preparation by the conductor.

Failure to Relate Note Length to March Style

Failure to achieve correct style frequently occurs in the performance of a standard march. The concept of spacing and the marcato style is often overlooked and misunderstood. Only occasionally does a band perform this style of music with too much space between notes.

March melodies which start with eighth note pickups are frequently played without separation. Rhythm patterns which combine sustained tones with short note values are usually all played in a sustained style. Dotted eighths and sixteenths, while sometimes played with too much separation, are more frequently performed with weight on the wrong note. Instead of placing the weight on the note which falls on the first part of the beat, the sixteenth note comes out stronger as a result of an effort to make it short, thereby giving the pattern an awkward rhythmic inflection.

Inability to Prioritize Melody, Harmony, and Accompaniment

In interpreting the march, a conductor must constantly assess the importance of musical lines and ensembles within the score to establish correct musical priorities. Accompanying voices in the break strain of the traditional march are often played too loudly. Such parts are all marked "ff," but common musical sense should tell us that the melodic line in the low brass is more important than repetitive accompanying figures in treble voices. Good judgment in balancing sustained accompaniment with melody and countermelody becomes the mark of a good musician, but simple evaluation of which voice must project over others is a skill within reach of all conductors.

The Fugue

A prime example of characteristic problems in lack of clarity between voices and ensembles is the prelude and fugue form. A considerable number of these compositions by Bach have been transcribed and appear on contest lists. Bands tend to play all of the line at equal strength without an understanding of the importance of any of them.

The Legato, Normal, and Marcato

There are very few performances that would not profit from a clear distinction between normal and legato articulation. In contrast to staccato and marcato, the legato deficiency is not as easily diagnosed. The problem is rather easily understood. In either case there always seem to be a few players who understand and execute the correct note lengths, but especially in legato playing, there can be a large diversity of opinion about how to correctly achieve the intended effect. The maximum sustained effect from the wind band can only be achieved when the air stream is not terminated between notes, but rather, interrupted by an articulated effect of the tonguing mechanism. This effect can be achieved only when the articulation is accomplished without any distortion or change of the volume level between notes. It is only truly effective when correctly executed by upwards of 90% of the ensemble involved.

Failure to Understand the Phrase Line

Musically expressive phrasing seems to be one of the great mysteries in effective band performance. There is an obvious relationship between physical maturity in breath control and the ability to play complete musical phrases or ideas. However, careless or incorrect beginnings and endings of phrases frequently occur in groups who have achieved such maturity. Fragmentation of musical lines is often observed in less-advanced groups. The problem is encouraged by scores which show phrases slurred in two-measure segments, when in reality, the musical thought actually continues for four to eight measures. Such is frequently the case in Grade I and II literature and the conductor would be wise to edit the parts to achieve a more satisfactory effect.

Mature ensembles with adequate facility to sustain complete phrases often perform ineffectively because they have not been made aware of motion, intensity, and subtle dynamic changes which are not indicated on the score, but are so essential in creating a musical effect. Music of the Romantic period suffers most when these elements in phrasing are neglected, but even Baroque and Classical music must have direction and a sense of movement in progressing through the musical idea.

Problems of Intensity and Dynamics in Phrasing

It is a safe assumption in the origination of every musical phrase that, at some point in the progression of the phrase, there will be some variation in the intensity and dynamic levels of at least some of the notes in the written line. In a few exceptional cases, the exact opposite will be true, but that will be a matter of design and will be a relatively rare occurrence. A general practice of building intensity to the highest note in the phrase is a good starting assumption, but very often the exact opposite of that practice turns out to be more musically correct. Phrase segments which repeat one or more times always demand variation or reinforced intensity with such repetition.

The human voice is good as a role model for illustrative purposes; it helps to explore the question: "How would this sound if it were vocalized or even put to words?"

Variations in Tempo Within and Between Measures

Use of the rubato, accelerando, and ritard are more obvious devices for motion in phrasing. There seems to be a great reluctance for conductors to use these important musical devices. The problem emanating from the lack of such tempo adjustments is often rooted in a lack of confidence in basic conducting skills. Many conductors feel the musical need for the rubato but are unable to activate and control the changes without losing control of the ensemble. Additionally, in such cases the material has been rehearsed and "learned" at one tempo which prohibits further flexibility from the ensemble.

Ritards are more easily affected since they involve only a slowing down of the music. However, the importance of slowing each beat and subdivision in a cumulative or progressively slower tempo is often overlooked. Such groups simply regress from the "a tempo" to one that is uniformly slower at the conclusion of the phrase or segment.

Abuse of the Fermata

An effective interpretation of the length of the fermata is seldom heard in any but the most musically mature bands. As a starting point, one general rule for the length of the fermata provides the addition of one-half of the original value to the note. Such application can require either more length or less; however, the usual practice is to detract time from the potential length of the fermata, thereby minimizing the possible musical effect.

In view of the fact that the fermata is an intended pause in the music, it is a first responsibility of the conductor to seek out the reason for a pause. Such a reason can include emphasis of the sound over which the fermata is indicated, anticipation of a contrasting tempo or style which is to follow, or simply a point of punctuation between two musically related or unrelated ideas. From that standpoint, it is extremely important for the conductor to use the proper amount of time required for the fermata to have the desired effect. Quite often, the ensemble is completely ineffective because the individual players are unprepared to sustain a good quality of sound for an appropriate length of time. Instead of preparing the ensemble to sustain the fermata, the conductor approaches this point with trepidation, knowing that neither he nor the band know exactly what to expect.

Failure to Perform at Correct Tempos

There are many good and musically acceptable reasons for bands to perform literature at tempos which do not exactly adhere to those marked on the score. The most valid such reason is that the indicated tempos are normally "suggested tempos" which can be marginally altered if it does not detract from the intended purpose by the composer. In contradiction to this statement, there are certain band composers who reflect very positive restrictions in tempo which they indicate on their scores and usually say so in the conductor's notes. In such cases, these metronome markings serve to govern the total framework of a movement or composition to assure the performance of a major climax point or section at exactly the right tempo for maximum effect. The application of good musical judgment in a gradual succession of tempo changes that logically leads to the only tempo at which such a given section will be effective.

Unfortunately the reasons given above are seldom the ones which contribute to errors in tempo judgment. Most often, tempos are adjusted downward so that bands can manage the technical demands of the performance; such is often the case in the performance of some of the great Classical and Romantic works transcribed for band. Admittedly, it is possible to make such adjustments and still achieve a good musical performance, but more often the conductor who is faced with such a concession would do well to select literature which can be performed at a correct or desirable tempo with the given technical skills available.

Unplanned Tempo Changes

The unforgivable errors in tempo are those which develop as a result of loss of control by the conductor. This loss of control happens with marches that start frantically and gradually wind down to the correct tempo or one that is too slow. It is also a characteristic of a Largo or Adagio tempo, which gradually accelerates.

Band conductors fail to take advantage of contrasting sections of a piece which are marked "Allegro" and "Moderato Sostenuto." These, or similar contrasting indicators, often appear on easier band literature and are intended to provide the conductor with musical license for an interesting performance. All too often the "Allegro" section does not achieve its potential in lightness and clarity. The contrasting "sostenuto" section continues in the same style instead of a connected legato style which would lend the desired contrast.

Misunderstanding of Form

The failure to understand musical form and properly interpret the various segments is not unusual by conductors of bands at all maturity levels. The Suite is one of the most employed forms of literature in all grade levels. From the "Little English Suite" by Leroy Jackson on Grade I to the "Suite of Old American Dances" by Robert Russell Bennett on Grade V, the opportunities for performance of this musical form are without limit. Similarly, the Texas *University Interscholastic League* list shows numerous collections of "dances" which are performed throughout the country. More mature musical organizations perform complete symphonies and other major multimovement works by composers including Hindemith, H. Owen Reed, Grainger, Nelhybel, and many others.

Problems of Key, Style, and Tempo Relationship

Regardless of the designation of the form or its difficulty, every band conductor who chooses to program such a work has a common problem. An assessment of the musical reasoning underlying each segment must be made in terms of style, tempo, key relationship, and melodic and ensemble content. Those factors which determine contrast and interest must be identified. An error frequently heard from young bands is the performance of all three movements of a suite in the same nondescript style, tempo, and dynamic level. In many cases the conductor must develop a vivid musical imagination in the presentation of simple music material with appropriate contrasting style and tempos. Even in music of the most elementary level, to do less than that is a complete abdication of musical responsibilities.

Similar considerations apply to the musical performance of many single-movement works such as overtures and tone poems. The opportunities for contrast and music interest must be studied and exploited. Such musical needs reinforce the importance of teaching which provided the skills for simple variety of note length and dynamic levels as a basic requirement for each and every student.

BIBLIOGRAPHY

"Band Music Guide," *The Instrumentalist,* (1970).

Bird, John. *Percy Grainger.* (London: Elek Books Limited, 1976)

Fennell, Frederick. "Basic Band Repertory: British Band Classics from the Conductor's Point of View," *The Instrumentalist,* (1980).

Lobuta, Joseph A. *Teaching Musicianship in the High School Band.* (West Nyack, NY: Parker Publishing Company, Inc., 1975)

Prescribed Music List. (Austin, TX: University Interscholastic League, 1983)

Westrup, J. A., and F. L. Harrison. *The New College Encyclopedia of Music.* (New York, NY: W. W. Norton and Company, Inc., revised 1976)

12

The Marching Band

No single musical organization in the public schools, colleges, or universities is seen by as many people as the marching band. In many cases, a single performance by the school marching band is viewed by more spectators than all of the concerts in the same year. The average citizen and school patron quite often arrives at an assessment of the total music program in the school based on his impression of the marching band in a parade or at an athletic contest. Major decisions to provide financial support for school band programs are frequently influenced by the need for school and community service by the marching band.

Financial support which benefits the total band program in secondary and higher education often originates as a direct result of service to athletic-connected events. The large marching bands serving colleges and universities are frequently supported totally or in part by athletic funds. These funds provide travel, food, and lodging, and assist in providing uniforms, equipment, and scholarship support for members of the marching band, and indirectly for the entire band program. Similar parallels may be drawn from conditions in the public school.

A review of the foregoing facts often produces a philosophical conflict in the minds of band conductors who accept the responsibility of the total band program. It is not difficult to understand a certain resistance to the training of the marching band which demands such a major part of the school year and seems to produce minimal opportunities for musical development and expression. However, without fail, the first annual responsibility of the band director in most situations is the assembly, organization, and training of the largest single group of students involved in the band program for the purpose of multiple performances for outdoor events. Since such a condition is unalterably universal and is likely to remain so, it becomes imperative that this activity exists as a musical endeavor and that it be directed by a person with a mature and enthusiastic outlook to the entire process.

PRIORITIES IN THE DEVELOPMENT OF THE MARCHING BAND

The primary condition upon which to base the development of the marching band is that it *must teach musical skills*. The conditions under which musical skills may be taught in the marching band are many, and will be discussed. A second objective or purpose of the marching band lies in the fact that it is the ideal vehicle for teaching concomitant values such as discipline, teamwork, responsibility, and leadership. A third and more functional objective demands that the marching band be a source of entertainment. This objective is a somewhat standard application for music of all types and quality. Music is an art form which holds value to the consumer as well as the creator. It may not be entirely inappropriate for students in the public schools to become aware that the high cost of a quality music program can be supported in part through their efforts which do not necessarily result in the performance of the best in literature. The calibre of music which entertains a football audience is not always of lasting value, but it is characteristic of the world around us and the kinds of music which make up the total spectrum.

The purpose of the marching band, then, may be stated as follows:

1. The training and organization of the marching band must teach musical skills.

2. The training and organization of the marching band must capitalize on the opportunities to teach concomitant values such as discipline, leadership, and responsibility through group participation.

3. The performance of the marching band must serve to entertain patrons at athletic events and perhaps even inspire participants in competition. Such performances are not limited to athletics, but can include parades, concerts, and competitive marching events.

At this point it is important to emphasize that the three purposes set forth do have a definite order of priority. If the order should become inverted or rearranged, the marching band program can no longer be considered educationally sound or defensible. If any of the three purposes is not effectively carried forth, the health and balance of the marching band will fall into question. The director of bands or band conductor charged with this responsibility who cannot enthusiastically support or affect a program with these objectives is doing a disservice to the students under his leadership.

CONTRIBUTING TO THE DEVELOPMENT OF THE MUSICIAN

Teaching musical skills through the marching band starts by first identifying those skills which are important to any kind of performance. These skills include:

1. Playing with good tone quality and balance
2. Controlling effective dynamic ranges
3. Developing breathing and support habits
4. Playing with good intonation, correct style, and rhythm

Tone Quality and Control

The importance of teaching public school students to maintain good tone quality as wider ranges of dynamics are developing becomes a major challenge. The temptation to accept bad sound and the accompanying damage to embouchures in exchange for louder dynamics is easy to understand. Outdoor band fans react favorably to increased decibels. They are generally limited in judging poor tone quality and hence do not react adversely when this characteristic accompanies the bigger sounds. More powerful sound levels are certainly desirable but the preparation and development of such skills must be done under the watchful eye of a competent director.

The development of better breathing and support habits can be a natural product of marching band training. In an activity where everything is more physical, it is only logical to encourage and require deeper breathing to sustain more and better sound outdoors. For that reason, it is much more productive to conduct rehearsals outdoors where the band can be seated and reasonably protected from the elements.

Teaching Intonation

There is no reason to avoid daily tuning at the beginning of the marching band rehearsal. The band should always begin each rehearsal in a predetermined formation which permits good rehearsal discipline by the conductor. A regular warm-up procedure including unison and octave tuning exercises is entirely appropriate at the beginning of each rehearsal. Many directors find it helpful to initiate a moving warm-up procedure which lets the band move down the field with the yard lines while playing a scale or other warm-up exercises. In addition to providing listening opportunities for tuning and physical warm-up for the embouchure, it also emphasizes accuracy of stride.

Rhythmic Accuracy and Phrasing

During actual rehearsal of program material, the importance of proper execution, rhythmic accuracy, and good phrasing is important, as in any performance preparation. The challenge of marching band arrangements can be equally as demanding as that for the concert band. Good phrasing must be monitored very carefully. In the process of developing strong dynamic levels, students tend to need more breath, and often fragment phrases in order to breathe frequently. It is not uncommon to hear bands at the university level who breathe after each measure to achieve dynamic projection. This practice may serve quite well to cheer the team on to victory, but is not a desirable habit for maturing school musicians.

Supporting the Development of Woodwinds

The role of the woodwind section in the marching band is the most critical of all. The practice of transferring all woodwinds to flags, rifles, batons, or other auxiliary activities will not help their musical skills. In this respect, it would be much better to develop such auxiliary groups from nonplaying students. A second alternative is to set certain individual playing standards which must be met before a student could be considered for an auxiliary position. This group should be afforded some opportunity to remain active playing their instrument on at least a limited basis throughout the marching season.

The woodwind choir in the marching band is threatened when trying to compete for levels which would balance with the brass and percussion sections. It is not unusual for woodwinds to begin using exaggerated force in tonguing under such conditions. Admittedly, the marching band ensemble must accommodate a louder, more powerful brass and percussion sound in relation to traditional concert band-ensemble concepts. However, the woodwind section must maintain its identity as a balanced choir. A director can encourage this skill by more prudent and careful selection of music. Continued use of standard marches with meaningful woodwind parts in the stands is recommended. Band arrangements which score some independence for woodwinds will be helpful, and any contest performance will profit from the contrast afforded by this practice.

There will be occasions when the band that employs all of the safeguards in developing musical skills will be "upstaged" by visiting bands which break all of the rules of good musical judgment. The applause sometimes goes to the loudest band. Conductors and bands who are working toward furthering musical skills may need to remind themselves of the importance of developing the total musician. These values often surface the following spring when the efforts of the concert band are rewarded by such disciplined philosophy.

MARCHING BAND STYLES

There are at least three distinct styles of marching performance which have a historical identity, and their development can be traced almost from their origin. Although a lengthy historical treatment would not serve a useful purpose at this point, knowledge about the point of origin can be helpful in anticipating the future of style in the marching band. The three basic styles to be discussed are the Precision Drill, the Show Band, and the Drum and Bugle Corps.

Precision Drill

Precision drill for marching bands was originally confined to those bands which marched in a military style, using the 30-inch stride. These groups did not necessarily adhere to multiples of steps which corresponded to yard lines on the gridiron because the practice of marking each five yards on the football field is a relatively recent innovation. The tempo was naturally limited to a range of 100 to 126 mm. The heel contacted the ground initially on each step. Standard military marches were performed exclusively.

Bands doing predominantly precision-drill maneuvers also included those who utilized the 22½-inch step which corresponded to eight equal subdivisions of the five-yard intervals on the football field. This type of movement originated in conjunction with a high knee lift and the toe or front part of the foot contacting the ground initially on each step. By shortening the length of the step to this size it became possible to move at tempos much faster than the traditional military style, and expanded the potential musical repertoire to include not only marches, but popular tunes as well.

Precision drill is characterized as that style which allows or demands identification and location of every member of the marching unit on every measure and beat of movement during a performance. The emphasis is upon exact adherence to the dimensions of the performance area and precise execution of movement within these confines.

Show Band Style

The show band style often employed certain features of precision drill and generally moved with the high knee lift and the 22½-inch step. The format of the performance however was quite different. The musical selections usually were based on a show theme and formations reinforcing this theme were outlined by bandsmen on the field. As this style became more popular, movement, action, and props were introduced for a more colorful effect. The emphasis was on entertainment and the performance usually was supported by an elaborate script leading the spectators through the sequence of formations and melodies.

Drum and Bugle Corps Style

The drum and bugle corps style is more commonly referred to as simply the "Corps" style. Its origin dates back to community groups with volunteer leadership who worked together on weekends. Their rehearsals took place on any convenient open area which was available, usually a baseball field, parking lot, or open field. This important point of origin gave the Corps a flexibility which was not tied to points of reference like the football field yard lines or hash marks.

Until recent years the Drum and Bugle Corps did not enjoy great respect among serious marching performers. The sounds of drums and bugles were unrefined and had severe musical limitations because of the mechanical design. Membership was voluntary and the purpose was generally of a recreational and social nature. Those in charge of organizing and rehearsing the groups did so in the spirit of community service for boys and girls, although the corps was usually confined to members of the male sex.

Since 1970, the Drum Corps have dramatically evolved into some of the most effective mobile performing units in existence. Through the encouragement of *Drum Corps International* and financial support of dedicated community organizations, the leadership of these corps includes some of the best-qualified wind and percussion experts in the country. Presented suddenly with a new forum for their skills, talented arrangers began writing special music for a vastly improved family of "bugles," ranging from a newly designed bass bugle through the entire register of tonal possibilities. These performing groups incorporated elaborate and expertly choreographed "lines" of flags and rifles to add to the impact of the total musical effect. An effective organization of summer travel and performance across the country, culminating in world final competition, captured the admiration and envy of all but the most skeptical leadership in the marching band world.

Most band directors will concede that the advent of the modern "Corps" has given marching bands a new direction. The flexibility of both movement and music can be put to good advantage in the traditional marching band. The length of stride employed by traditional corps is best described as "seven to five," somewhere in between the 22½-inch and the 30-inch stride. However, within the fundamentals of corps marching there lies a vast variety of step size permitting movement to all tempos and styles of music in the same performance. The underlying principle of the corps style bases all movement on the premise that it must enhance or interpret the music.

Indirectly, then, one of the most influential characteristics which historically influenced the style of marching units has been *tempo.* School bands which began in the military tradition functioned quite effectively until their purpose began to include the need for entertainment. This need resulted in the performance of music at tempos faster than the march. The band then had to make the decision to stop marching in order to perform the music or change the length of stride to continue marching at the faster tempo. Most college bands were faced with the responsibility of performing spirited school and "fight" songs which could only move with shorter steps. The addition of the knee lift and bodily movement evolved in a natural rhythmic support of such tempos and eventually became known as the "Big Ten" style.

The drum corps of today perform music of every conceivable tempo. Instead of limiting themselves to the six-to-five and eight-to-five movements, they match the stride to the desired tempo and tailor the style of the movement to the style of the music. Many marching bands have integrated certain of these features into a basic style which best fits their needs. Since bands continue to perform primarily on football gridirons, it seems foolish to abandon the traditional checkpoints of yard lines and hash marks. These checkpoints continue to aid the execution and uniformity of a performance, even when combined with other flexible features of the corps style.

The advent of curvilinear forms and movement has added another dimension to marching band performances. Patterns and formations which were formerly limited to straight or diagonal lines now have the expanded capabilities of the arc or curve. Many bands are able to master the fundamental of both kinds of movement and present a dramatic and flexible performance format.

PRELIMINARY PLANNING FOR THE MARCHING SEASON

Every band director responsible for the performance of the marching band in the school music program is faced with certain decisions related to proper preparation for the fall marching season. There are decisions which must be made but can be approached well in advance of the season with proper reflection and planning or delayed until conditions make the entire process a frustrating and disorganized part of the school year. These decisions have at some time been made by every director, regardless of maturity or tenure, and in such cases are reviewed regularly, although the entire process is much more orderly and controlled. Under normal circumstances, this kind of planning should be done methodically and before the pressure of other events, such as organizing beginner classes, is present.

Basic Style

The basic style of the marching band will speak for the total music program. As pointed out previously, certain school patrons will formulate their total opinion on the basis of the performance of the marching band. The election of a basic style must support the avowed criteria for teaching music. The marching band should uphold the dignity and worth of the music program. It should support and promulgate social values and provide the opportunity to support the principals of discipline as well as teach students to be good leaders. It should take on the functional role of entertainment in good taste with the presentation of students in auxiliary groups as well as the wind and percussion players in making good sounds and supporting movement. All of these must be considered in the selection and assessment of the marching style.

The length of stride for most bands includes the 22½-inch step. Whether it is combined with the knee lift, confined to a corps style "glide step," or simply used in a walking style, this step must be considered in conjunction with other features of the kinds of performance planned. Adherence to a strict corps style will dictate the glide step. The walking stride is a modification more easily taught and conforms well to the use of the 30-inch stride for variety of movement. The knee lift is considered more traditional and difficult to control without disturbing the upper torso and embouchure.

Performance that incorporates additional movement such as dance steps and hand and arm motion must be carefully planned and detailed from a fundamental standpoint. Uniform execution of such motion requires careful presentation and teaching in the basic training of each member of the marching band.

Basic Formation

The basic formation of the marching band must serve the following important needs:

1. It should be a starting place for each rehearsal, providing for easy location and identification of each bandsman for roll-check and other organizational purposes.

2. It should provide a satisfactory grouping of instruments for warm-up and playing rehearsal and review, and placement of the percussion section and auxiliaries.

3. It should provide for the strategic location of student leaders who can assist in roll-check, tuning, and disseminating information as well as the easy removal of a segment of students for separate training.

4. It should convert easily to a performance position or parade block.

An important consideration when deciding on the basic formation is the proper placement of the instruments for the best musical potential. Such a formation will usually be some type of rectangular block in a predetermined position on the field and at a specified interval. Instruments which play basic rhythm or "beat" parts such as tubas, percussion, bass clarinet, and baritone saxophone should have a central location where their sound travels to the perimeter extremes at approximately the same time. This effect would not take place if the percussion were placed at the extreme right or left of the rest of the band. They are more ideally located in the middle back of the winds.

A basic formation arranged for maximum projection of sound will have the brasses in forward positions with woodwinds in back or the outside perimeter. A band which strives to continue to a more concert-oriented control and sound will have the woodwinds in front similar to seating of the concert band. It is well to anticipate the kind of drills which will be incorporated into performances so that the arrangement and grouping of instruments can be simulated in the basic formation. Bands which employ the format of locating the tubas and percussion at mid-field limiting their movement in the channel formed between the 45 yard lines enjoy a minimum of tempo problems. Figures 12-1 through 12-4 show several possible formations.

Standard Interval and Stride Length

The interval of the basic block must of course be predicated upon the size of the step or stride utilized in movement during the performance. Groups which plan to employ traditional lateral block marching will enjoy maximum security at a 60-inch interval if using the 30-inch step, or the 90-inch interval when using the 22½-inch step. The 45-inch interval in block movement is not advisable since it

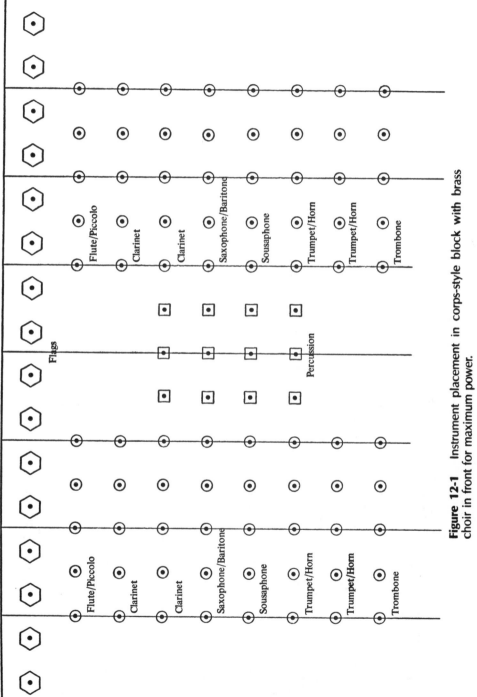

Figure 12-1 Instrument placement in corps-style block with brass choir in front for maximum power.

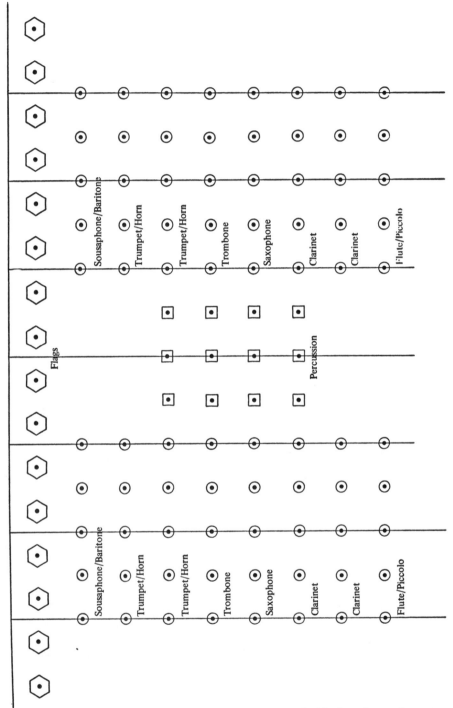

Figure 12-2 Instrument placement in corps-style block with wood-wind choir in front for concert balance emphasis. In performance, the percussion normally move to the front or back, permitting the winds to close the block.

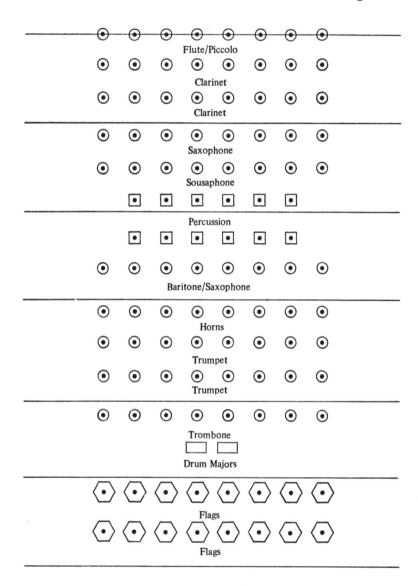

Figure 12-3 Traditional block with percussion ensemble. Brass choir in front for maximum projection.

Flags may be placed behind block for attractive border effect.

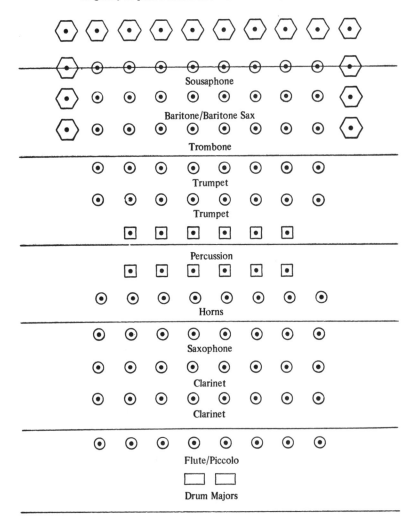

Figure 12-4   Traditional block with percussion ensemble. Woodwind choir in front for concert balance emphasis. Block is shown here at three-pace interval which is often more effective for parade marching although four-pace interval (90″) is customary for football field placement.

is too crowded for either good appearance or adequate maneuvering space. Such an interval in line or company front movement is, of course, quite common. In general, those bands using the 22½-inch step exclusively specify placement of individuals in a block at the 90-inch, or four-pace, interval. Bands using the 30-inch stride can work effectively with individuals placed at either the 60-inch (two-pace) or 120-inch (four-pace) interval in a block formation.

Auxiliary Units

Auxiliary Units used in conjunction with marching band performances may include (1) majorettes and feature twirler, (2) a flag line, (3) a rifle line, (4) a dance or drill team, and (5) optional separate grouping of the percussion ensemble. The band director would best limit the number of such auxiliary units to those for which adequate training and leadership can be sensibly provided. Many bands utilize extensive and sophisticated flag and rifle lines that have also mastered excellent dance skills under the supervision of a competent teacher. Every auxiliary unit named above requires some kind of separate and individual instruction to be a truly effective part of a performance. Student leadership can often be developed within each of these groups and function quite effectively throughout the performance season. Specialists may be imported for brief, intensive, training sessions during the summer or the units can be transported to separate camps for such specialized training. Regardless of what arrangements are made, the units must be exposed to good training and receive competent supervision during the year in order to be a worthy part of the total organization.

Marching Fundamentals

The formulation of a comprehensive set of fundamentals is perhaps *the* most important preparatory decision for successfully teaching the marching band. After decisions about style, interval, and auxiliary units have been finalized, the competent teacher must effectively capsulize the year-long needs of movement for the marching units and detail their execution and teaching. The teacher with some experience can more easily look back to a former marching season to evaluate exact needs which should be included in a manual for fundamental movement training. The new teacher must have a rather concrete and detailed impression of the kinds of movement to be required for performance in order to detail exact needs. In such cases, it is common to list and teach more fundamental movements than are actually needed. A summary of individual and group fundamentals is listed. As decisions are being made about which ones are to be included and how they shall be executed, the teacher should begin to develop a concept of limits of movement, refining all activity to basic movement which can be explained and easily taught and which may apply to more than one or two fundamentals.

The following list of fundamentals has been developed and used over a period of years. These fundamentals constitute a combination of movement originally based on military tradition and certain modifications which made them more applicable to contemporary use. The list can be adopted in its entirety or used as a checklist for the development of a more individualized manual upon which to base the training of the marching unit. It should be noted that certain movements detailed below are not appropriate for auxiliary units, especially not percussion.

1. *Parade Rest:* Heels 12 inches apart; toes moderately slanted out; body erect with shoulders and head back; eyes focused slightly above horizon. Left hand, with fingers closed and extended, is placed in center of back just below belt line; wrist remains straight but not stiff. Fingers of right hand (if not holding instrument) are slightly curved with thumb along seam of trousers. No talking or movement. Bandsman will assume this position before coming to "Attention" any time after the group has been ordered to fall in.

   Command "Puh-rade (silent beat) Rest!" (Lift left foot on first beat, place it down on next beat)

2. *Attention:* Héels together; toes approximately six inches apart. Body erect but not rigid. Shoulders back; head erect; eyes slightly above horizon. Instrument in "Carry" position.

   Command: "Band (silent beat) Ha-ten Hut!" (Lift, down) (Some bandsmen, especially cornet, trombones, etc. come to Parade Rest on the command "Band" or "Squad" *with instrument down.)* Raise horn, drop left hand, move left foot at same instant on *first pulse beat after* "Hut."

3. *At Ease:* Right foot remains in place; left foot moves out 12 inches at 45° angle. Body weight is shifted to right foot; left hand rests extended on left foreleg. Instrument may be lowered to a relaxed position.

   Command: "Stand (silent beat) Hadeze!" (Lift, down)

4. *At Rest:* Sit, kneel, or stand. Limited movement within a two square pace area. Talk if you care to. No horseplay. Instrument may be lowered or removed from carrier.

   Command: "A-a-t Hrest!"

5. *Fall In:* Find your predesignated place at a position of attention. After initial explanation of movements, this command will signify the beginning of each drill period.

   Command "Fall-in!"

6. *Fall Out:* Bandsman is released from drill period and assignment unless otherwise designated. Command may be preceded by instruction for relocation or reassignment during drill or rehearsal period. Command should be given from position of "Attention."

   Command: "Fall-out!"

7. *Present Horns:* A two-count maneuver executed prior to playing. On "one" the free hand moves sharply onto the instrument; on "two," the instrument arrives at playing position.

   Command: "Present (silent beat) Horns!" (Grip horn on 1, raise it up on 2.) This fundamental may also be a one-count movement when the instrument is at "Ready" position:

   Command: "Present (silent beat) Horns!" (up)

8. *Horns High:* A one-count maneuver usually executed during the performance for the purpose of sound projection. The instrument is shifted sharply up to a 45° angle on a beat before playing the first note to be projected upward. The angle may be adjusted to a specific target such as the press box.

   Horns Low: Same principle as above. Instruments are pointed at an angle towards the marching surface. On both of the above maneuvers, bandsmen who do not have bell front projection instruments will simulate movement for uniformity.

9. *Facing Movements:* Right Face, Left Face, Half-Right Face, Half-Left Face, About Face.

   a. *Right Face:* A four-count movement beginning with the standard "kick-step." On first pulse-beat after command, left foot kick-steps: foot hits the ground on two; pivot 90° to the right on ball of right foot and left toe on three; return heels together on four.

      Command: "Ra-hite (silent beat) Face!" (kick)

b. *Left Face:* Right foot kick-steps on one: foot hits ground on two; pivot 90° to the left on ball of left foot and right toe on three; return heels together on four.

Command: "Lay-efft (silent beat) Face!" (kick)

c. *About Face:* Left foot kick-steps on one; strike ground in line with right foot on two; pivot 180 degrees on ball of right foot and left toe on three; return heels together on four.

Command: "Habout (silent beat) Face!" (kick)

10. *Forward March:* When marching "six to five," the first movement is "kick step" made on first beat after the command with left leg straightened out directly ahead. Toe is held down close to the ground; heel strikes ground first. In marching "eight to five," left knee lifts up on the first beat; toe points down. The toe always strikes ground first.

Command: "Forwud (silent beat) March!"

11. *Stride/Step:* The standard "six-to-five stride" is a basic military gait. It is either 30 inches or 32 inches (when marching at the diagonal). It always begins with a "kick-step." The "eight-to-five step" is 22½ inches and may be used with either the "kick-step" or the "knee lift." When used with the knee lift, it continues with a moderate lift and careful pointing of the toe achieved by bending the ankle as the foot leaves and approaches the ground. This step will be designated as "Marching eight to five." When using eight to five in "Corps Style," the step is designated "Walking eight to five" and starts with the "kick step-off." The foot hits the ground with the heel first and continues with the regular appearance of six to five. In any of the three above styles of marching, all movement is concentrated from the waist down. The upper torso must remain steady to prevent any interference with basic playing functions.

12. *Halt:* Forward motion ceases on right foot. Bring left foot beside right from six inches directly above spot where heels should rest.

Command: "Squad (silent beat) Halt!" (R, L)

13. *Mark Time:* March in place in eight-to-five style. Toes leave the ground last, and come down first. Bend knee enough to lift foot directly over standing position with heel just below the kneecap of opposite leg to gauge height.

Command: "Mark Time (silent beat) March!" (Lift)

14. *Flank Movements:*

a. *Left-Flank:* A two-count movement beginning on the right foot on count two. On the "and" of two, pivot sharply to the left 90 degrees and step-off in new direction on next beat.

Command: "Left Flank (silent beat) March!"

b. *Half-Left:* Same as above but pivot only 45 degrees in the new direction.

Command: "Half-Left (silent beat) March!"

c. *Right-Flank:* A two-count movement beginning on the left foot on count one. On the "and" of one, pivot sharply to the right 90 degrees and step-off in new direction on next beat.

Command: "Right Flank (silent beat) march!"

d. *Half-Right:* Same as above but pivot only 45 degrees in the new direction.

Command: "Half-Right (silent beat) March!"

e. *Right Flank Halt:* Execute regular flank movement but leave left foot in place after pivot and bring right foot down sharply beside it.

f. *Left Flank Halt:* Execute regular flank movement but leave right foot in place after pivot and bring foot down sharply beside it.

g. *Cross to the Right:* Forward motion ceases on the right foot. Lift left foot, point toe down, bend knee, and kick to the right, pulling the body around on the "and" of the beat. (Be sure to remain faced in the old direction until the kick occurs on the "and" of the beat.)

Command: "Cross To The Right (silent beat) March!"

h. *Cross To The Left:* Forward motion ceases on left foot. Lift right foot with toe down, bend knee, and kick to the left, pulling the body around on "and" of the beat.

Command: "Cross to the Left (silent beat) March!"

15. *Column Left:* A movement which changes the bandsman's direction 90° to the left. The point of execution for each person in a file is normally the same. The actual column movement consists of a left flank; the file continues in sequence as they arrive at the original point of execution. This movement may be preceded by either a column halt or a column "Left to the Rear." When

preceded by the halt, a normal left foot kick-off is used plus one additional step so that the flank comes on the right foot. Likewise, one added step after the to-the-rear is used for the same reason.

Command: Column Left (Silent beat) March!

Column Right: A movement which changes the bandsman's direction 90° to the right. The movement consists of a cross to the right flank, then continuing forward in the new direction. The bandsman leading the file sets the Point of Execution on the command of "Execution."

Command: "Column Right (silent beat) March!"

This movement may also be preceded by either a "Column Halt" or a "Column Left to the Rear." When preceded by the halt, a normal left foot kick-off is used and the flank executed as the left foot hits the ground. Likewise, the flank to the right is executed by the lead bandsman on the second count of the to-the-rear movement.

16. *To the Rear:* Left to the Rear March, To the Rear Halt, Standing to the Rear.

    a. *Left to the Rear March:* Pivot 180° to the left on the balls of both feet, with right foot forward; continue marching in new direction. The balls of both feet remain in contact with the ground on pivot.

    Command: "Left to the Rear (silent beat) March!"

    b. *To the Rear Halt:* (Left to the Rear unless otherwise specified). Pivot 180° to the left on the ball of the right foot; bring the left foot down sharply in place beside the right foot on the next beat with heels together and toes apart in the position of "Attention."

    Command: "Halt to the Rear (silent beat) Halt!"

    c. *Standing to the Rear:* Shift the full weight of the body to the right foot and step off to the rear to your left.

    Command: (From stationary position) "To the Rear (silent beat) March!"

17. *Drag Turn:* Change of direction 90° in four counts; similar to mark time but gradually pivot in direction of the turn in time to step in the direction indicated on count five. Heel remains centered on the line. Drag Turn To The Rear (180°) is executed in eight counts.

Command: "Drag to the Left (silent beat) March!" (Lift)

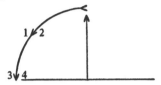

Command: "Drag to the Right (silent beat) March!" (Lift)

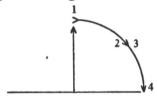

Command: "Drag to the Rear (Left) (silent beat) March!" (Lift)

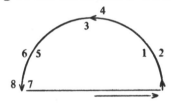

18. *Diagonal Marching:* Movement diagonally at a 45° angle between yard lines is accomplished by taking a slightly larger than regular 30-inch, six-to-five step (actually 32 inches). It is usually incorporated in a routine using basically eight to five steps at a slow tempo and must include a one-half or three-fourth flank movement in going from horizontal to diagonal movement. Use the 90-inch interval between bandsmen.

19. *Multi-Gait Marching:* A term used to indicate movement at several different-sized steps during the same maneuver, but by different bandsmen. It can include the 30-inch step at six to five; 22½-inch step at eight to five; 15-inch step at twelve to five; 11¼-inch step at sixteen to five; and the 7½-inch step at twenty-four to five. It is important for the bandsman to use a halfway sighting in pacing his motion.

20. *Follow-the-Leader Marching:* Following one bandsman in exact track and maintaining constant cover and interval.

21. *Bow Maneuvers:*

    a. *Waist Bow:* A seven-count maneuver beginning with the position of "Attention." Bow forward from waist at a 90° angle.

    Command: "Band Waist Bow!" (Bow on "one"; hold on counts "two" through "six"; up on "seven."

    b. *Neck Bow:* Same as above but drop head at neck. It may be combined with step-off. Raise head on "seven"; lift left foot on "eight"; step forward on "one" of new sequence.

BASIC LANGUAGE AND FOOTBALL FIELD DIMENSIONS

The terms of communication used in teaching marching band have become expanded with the advent of the corps style in public school work. Unfortunately, marching bands never have developed a standard repertoire of terms such as those which apply to musical scores and performance. The language of marching develops as the need arises and new techniques are implemented. A common directory of marching terms would be most helpful in exchanging information and promulgating the art. Even so, a somewhat understandable language has developed and students must be educated in the use of such language. Those terms such as file, rank, block, front, line, etc. must be introduced and explained to the extent that they apply to the fundamental style of marching that is used.

The dimensions of the marching band performance area, namely the athletic gridiron, are a much more common factor and must be thoroughly understood. The exact measurements of football fields are readily accessible, but it is interesting to note that many marching band directors do not always know or completely understand their use in marching performance.

Using Check Points

Standard procedure for school and college football requires that each five-yard line be marked across the 100-yard area between goal lines. In addition, the width of the field is divided into thirds with short "hash" marks on at least every ten-yard line. An "X" for the placement of the football on kickoff is designated on each 40-yard line at the exact midpoint between sidelines.

These standard checkpoints may be utilized in various ways and may be supplemented by additional checkpoints on practice areas which assist in the execution of individual drills. Circles, arcs, and other points can easily be chalked onto the surface of a rehearsal area. Bands using the 30-inch "six-to-five" stride can utilize the application of exactly 64 steps from one side line to the other. This distance coincidentally but conveniently corresponds to the number of counts in a standard march "trio" as well as other musical forms. The hash marks do not provide exact contact points but can be used to great advantage when properly understood. The chart in Figure 12-5 provides more specific information.

Distance in Length	Number of Steps				
	30-inch	22½-inch	Yards	Feet	Inches
1. Goal line to goal line	120	160	100	300	3600
2. End zone to end zone	144	192	120	360	4220
3. Each five yards	6	8	5	15	180
4. Each ten yards	12	16	10	30	360
5. To midfield (50 yard line)	60	80	50	150	1800

Distance in Width					
	30-inch	22½-inch	Yards	Feet	Inches
1. Sideline to sideline	64	84*	53⅓	160	1920
2. Sideline to 1st hash	21⅓	28*	17⅔	53⅓	640
3. Sideline to center	32	42*	26⅔	80	960
4. Sideline to 2nd hash	42⅔	56*	35⅓	106⅔	1280

*Adjusted to comply with "28-step system."

Figure 12-5 Standard check points.

The 22½-inch step seems to be in greater favor for a number of practical reasons. When moving laterally down the field, the eighth step corresponds to traditional musical phrasing. The size of the step is more manageable by younger marchers, and, of course, the flexibility in faster tempos becomes an all-important consideration.

The "28-Step" System

When applying eight-to-five marching to the vertical dimensions of the football field, some concessions in accuracy must be understood and made. Most bands adhere to a "28-step system" when moving vertically or parallel with the yard lines. In order to use the hash mark as a foot-contact point for the 28th step from the sideline or between hash marks in 28 steps, each step must be fractionally elongated. The actual distance is slight, amounting to .357 inch per 22½-inch step, but accumulates to a total of almost 30 inches when marching the total distance from sideline to sideline. The slight adjustment required to use the hash marks in this manner is a recommended practice and is easily mastered by students without much additional training. The common practice of vertical movement for maximum sound projection in contemporary drill makes this application very important.

Field Accuracy

When making use of field measurements, a first and necessary step is conducting a survey of the field with a tape measure to insure its accuracy or to become aware of any deviations. It is unusual to find a perfectly marked field, and a band can be spared many problems by the director who will take the time and trouble to acquaint them with any potential variations. Such a precaution is essential in surveying an actual contest site and makes the tape measure at least as important as the tuner for these events.

When using checkpoints, the ball of the foot is always the best and most specific part of the anatomy for contact placement. The student should be taught to march with the ball of the foot on the line and to sight down the middle when tracking a yard line. When tracking a sideline, however, the inner edge would be the track point. This practice minimizes any shift of the body that might result from pivots or other changes in direction.

PLANNING THE SHOW

Directing the performance toward the "home crowd" is common practice in planning marching band shows. This policy is generally acceptable for high school band work and applies to contest and festival performance when the primary impact is focused in one direction. The size of the home crowd and height of the stadium should serve to regulate the location of various parts of the performance in terms of distance from the sideline. Feature numbers and important action should be placed between the near hash mark and the sideline. Most high school stadiums concentrate the fans between the 20-yard lines and it is generally safe to focus the performance between the 30-yard lines. Climax and impact points should occur anywhere within the area ten to fifteen yards from the sideline. Smaller bands performing for smaller crowds should draw closer within that area. Action should generally stay within the confines of the sideline boundary.

Musical Content of the Show

The following points are helpful in planning a typical marching performance regardless of what style the band may employ:

1. Select the music, noting possible options for repeats, cuts, and modified endings. An average eight-minute performance can be developed from a minimum of three selections with the possibility of a short fanfare or opening selection, and a "closer" such as the school "fight" song.

2. Think the music through, noting which voice or ensemble carries the melody line, and identifying possible rhythmic and range problems, thin scoring, solo and soli voices, etc.

3. Consider the musical and melodic flow, accents, loud passages, soft contrasts, repeats, bridges, and vamps which may be suggestive of movement in the drill. Now make a "summary chart" (see Figure 12-6) of the selection, identifying briefly the characteristics of each segment or melodic strain. Note the exact number of counts in each segment and suggested tempi.

4. Continue study of the selection with a prepared tape recording. Consider patterns of movement and repetition which would fit what the music says. Look for ways to begin fitting segments of the music to the distance in steps between hash marks. Identify musical segments which should have priority to be heard most strongly as well as those which might serve to change direction, mood, or staging.

5. Look for a climax or surprise; emphasize musical accent or dynamic levels with motion. Finish the selection facing the audience.

Figure 12-6 Music Summary Sheet.

Saints - Bowles, Arr.
Title or sequence

Central vs. Tyler, Nov. 5
Game and date

MUSIC	SCORING	COUNTS	TAB	DRILL/FORMATION IDEAS	CHART
Saints					
Intro	Key of F and full ensemble	8		Wind block hold. Flags start restage.	
				Percussion starts restage.	
(5) Chorus	Trumpet lead	32		CF:A-K track FM + 8, column 16 DT 4.	
				CF:CM FM + 12 and consolidate.	
(21) Chorus in A♭	Trombone lead	16		All winds FM + 16. Then float 12 and DT 4;	
		16		Hold front (=32)	
(37) Interlude	Full ensemble	16		Percussion back. Flags continue 16.	
				Major to center and halt four.	
(45) Building	Pyramid	8		Major - flag routine to end.	
Intro. repeat		16			
(57) Last chorus	Antiphonal	16		Winds restage to outside arc.	
	Low brass	8		DT 4 and consolidate.	
Ending	Augmented time	22	𝄐	H-step + 8 in 16; horns high on 17.	
				Hold to end; release on 9.	

Physical Movement in the Show

Most movement or drill can be categorized into general types. These are a few examples:

1. Unison Drills: A change of direction or action simultaneously by an entire unit or group such as "Flank left," "Flank right," "To the Rear," and "Arc Expansion." Good for sudden impact.
2. Follow-the-Leader Drill· Movement by individuals that occurs at the same location, but in a regular sequence such as a column, countermarch, or tracking a curve or pattern.
3. Contagion Drill· A series of individuals moving in sequential order but not ın a pulse related to meter. These movements can be head movement, bows, and hand signals, and are especially suited to auxiliary groups.
4. Step-two Drill: Individual and small-group movement in metered tempo. This forms the basis for a variety of traditional precision drills. Can be altered to include step-one, step-four, etc. in any direction.
5. Circle Drill: Effective in rotation by tracking perimeter, and expansion and compression. May be modified to use only half circles similar to arcs.
6. Squad drills: Pinwheel and spinner movement; the "Patterns in Motion" concept.

DRILL CONSTRUCTION

Many band directors enjoy the kind of creative exercises required to originate and apply imaginative drill movement to music. Those who are not particularly adept at the art consider drill origination a curse and a bane, and usually the source of great frustration.

Necessary Equipment and Supplies

Most directors have certain creative abilities which will surface with practice and a reasonable investment of time. A first and most helpful step in constructing drill movement is the acquisition of adequate charting equipment and supplies. A wealth of printed charting paper and accompanying tools for contemporary drill design is readily available. Once the decision regarding basic style has been made, the acquisition of supplies that apply to that style must be made. It is often only a matter of time before the director gains enough experience to design and duplicate charts which apply more specifically to a given situation. Until then, the products which are commercially available can work very well.

Charting: Put Some Positions on Paper

A second valuable step in charting is to begin experimental assignment of the basic formations and auxiliaries to actual positions on the field. Attractive patterns should be worked up in five to ten different locations with various sections in prominent positions. During this process, things such as visual perspective from the stands and sound projection may be evaluated without any particular regard as to how the formation was derived. The application of certain formations and positions to music already selected may become apparent.

Visualize Some Movement

A third step in drill construction occurs as the movement to form and leave the charted positions becomes necessary. Certain combinations and sequences immediately may be eliminated because they are impractical, take too much time, and cause an appearance of disorder on the field. By the same token, however, certain movements which seem at first to take a great deal of time may develop into an orderly and interesting flow as the routes and procedure for movement are organized and detailed.

During this process of planning movement, a balance consisting of structured moves, which may be precision drill, and moves which simply restage the band, should be maintained. The complexity of such movement at the beginning of the marching season will be limited with more emphasis on playing performance. As the band begins to learn a repertoire and if time permits, more elaborate drills and movement will be added to the performance.

PLANNING FOR COMPETITION

The element of preparation for competition is a major factor in most marching band programs in the public schools. Some bands may anticipate competition in one or two events for the season while others look for a regular tour of contests similar to that of the Drum Corps. In the former case, such a band would plan to present a more diversified program of performances during the season or place considerably less emphasis on outdoor activities. The latter would probably work toward the development and perfection of a single show to the level of a major-level "final" competition. Either type of program has certain characteristics in common that require a gradual and ordered addition of features and drills to each successive performance.

Originating and Completing the Drill

Here are some additional guidelines which are helpful in drill construction:

1. Conceive an entire sequence of movement in a broad or general way before specifically applying it to segments of the music. In addition to knowing what musical effect is intended and how the ensemble can achieve this effect, have in mind where the drill originates and where it should terminate to lead into the next part of the performance.

2. Divide the drill into understandable and rehearsable segments that correspond to the music in exact counts and measures.

3. Subdivide the drill into the lowest or smallest teachable fragment. This fragment often turns out to be a fundamental from the manual or a series of such fundamentals to which the student can more easily relate.

4. Completed diagrams and charts for the entire drill must be available for teaching, but are not always necessary for each individual. Duplicate only that material which will save time and clarify points quickly. Remember that drills must be converted to memory.

5. All movement should be based on fundamentals detailed in the manual and taught at the beginning of marching season. Use a system of charting which shows a bandsman *where* he starts and *where* he finishes. *How* the student arrives at these locations must be explained verbally or through brief printed instructions that relate to fundamental movement.

6. Always record the drill version of the music as soon as possible before starting to polish the drill. Use of a cassette recorder which can play back at variable speeds is most helpful; the drill can then be taught at a slower tempo when necessary. In the countless repetition of movement normally required for a polished performance, the use of a previously prepared tape recording can save lips and preserve enthusiasm for a better musical presentation.

COMPUTERIZED CHARTING AIDS

The application of computers in the design and charting of drills has proven to be a valuable development for the marching band. Several charting programs are now available which dramatically reduce the man-hours formerly required to produce charted drills. Such computer programs instantly solve the tedious chore of accurate placement of positions in curves, arcs, circles, and other patterns, as well as straight lines. The subdivision of a curve or an arc into a specified interval of one, two, three, or more steps for any given number of positions can be instantly viewed on the screen and plotted on paper. Experimentation that takes hours to chart manually can now be plotted by the computer in minutes. The time and effort saved can be spent in creative planning rather than meticulously charting a design by hand which may not work.

In addition to the reproduction of static chart positions, some of the programs will plot and reproduce movement between forms in measured increments. Intermediate positions at four, eight, sixteen or more counts between beginning and ending positions may be shown.

Although the cost of the computerized charting aid is modest by standards of the industry, it may be beyond the means of accessibility for every school band director. It would be fair to point out that such a program is of greater value to one who must design drills for large numbers. Charting for a band of 40 to 60 winds with accompanying auxiliaries is still quite manageable using traditional tools by hand.

Figures 12-7 through 12-10 show four formations using a scale drawing of the football field, courtesy of The University of Arkansas Marching Razorback Band.

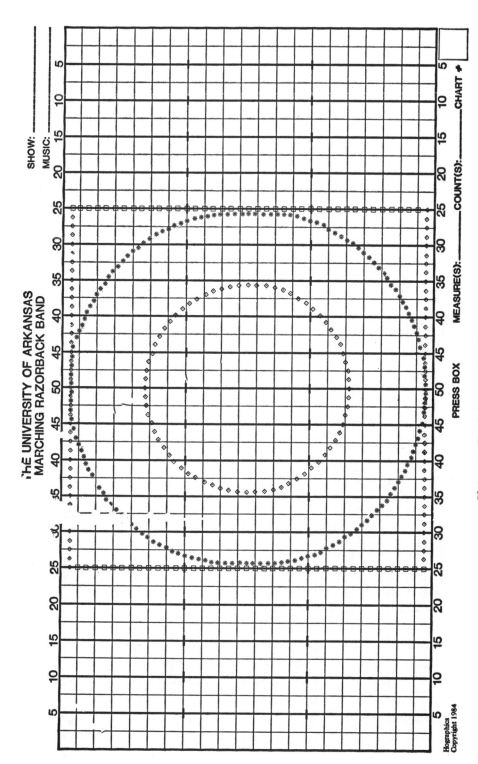

Figure 12-7 Square and circle formation.

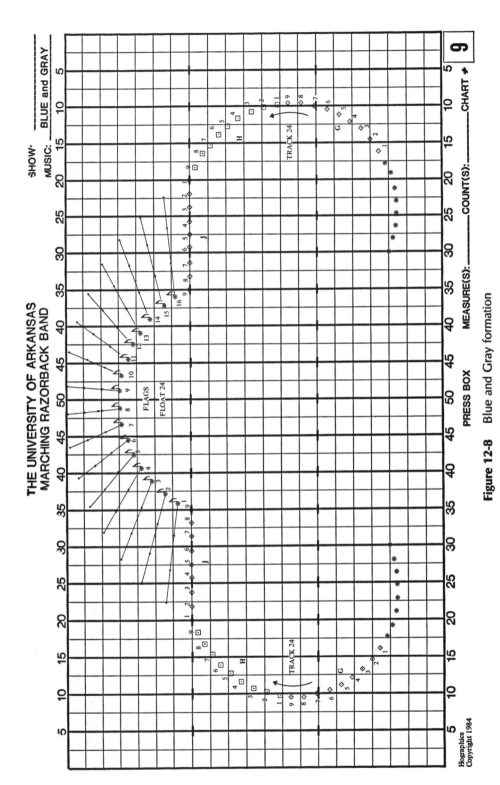

Figure 12-8 Blue and Gray formation

194

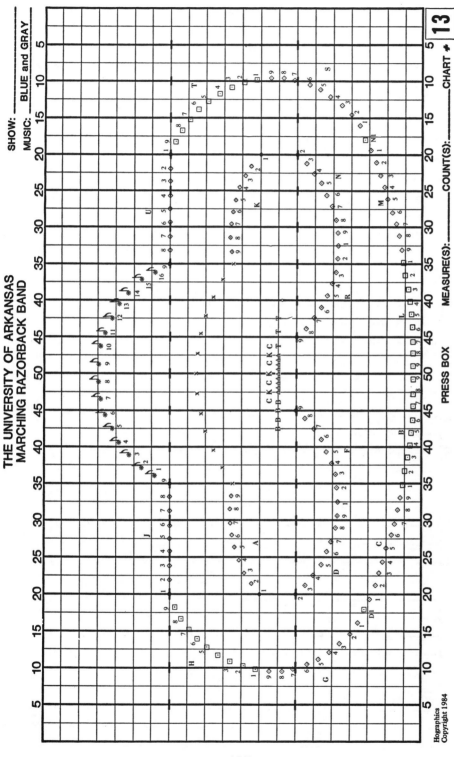

THE UNIVERSITY OF ARKANSAS
MARCHING RAZORBACK BAND

SHOW: _____

MUSIC: BLUE and GRAY

CHART # 13

COUNT(S): _____

MEASURE(S): _____

PRESS BOX

Figure 12-9   Blue and Gray formation.

Hographics
Copyright 1984

195

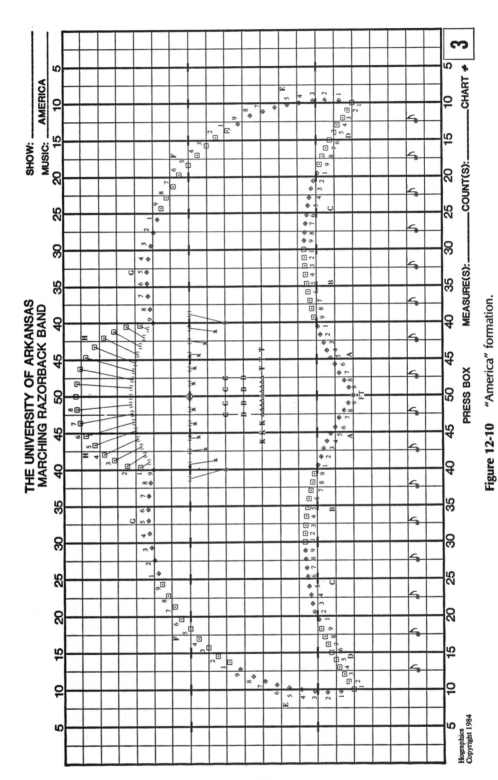

THE UNIVERSITY OF ARKANSAS
MARCHING RAZORBACK BAND

SHOW: _____
MUSIC: __ AMERICA __

MEASURE(S): _____ COUNT(S): _____ CHART # __3__

PRESS BOX

Figure 12-10 "America" formation.

Hographics
Copyright 1984

196

BIBLIOGRAPHY

Casavant, A. R. *Exhibition Marching* (five volumes). (Chattanooga, TN: ARC Products Company, 1975)

Hopper, Dale F. *Corps Style Marching.* (Oskaloosa, IA: C. L. Barnhouse Company, Music Publishers, 1977)

Moffit, Bill. *Patterns of Motion.* (Winoma, MN: Hal Leonard Music Inc., 1964)

Raxdale, Bill. *Contemporary Show Design Manual.* (New Berlin, WI· Jenson Publications, Inc., 1981)

Snoeck, Kenneth M. *Contemporary Drill Design.* (Oskaloosa, IA: C. L. Barnhouse Company, Music Publishers, 1981)

13

The Stage Band

The advent of the stage band into the established music curriculum is a relative recent concept in instrumental-music education. This ensemble, representing the true American art form of jazz, has had some difficulty gaining acceptance as a legitimate part of the music mission in the public schools, and it may be well to recognize some of the problems which have been traditionally connected with this facet of the music curriculum.

PURPOSE AND SIZE OF THE ENSEMBLE

It is also relevant to recognize the several concepts of what a "stage band" can mean in the public schools. The stage band can include any ensemble of standard instrumentation, from five saxes, six brass, and three rhythm, to that of both more or less ambitious proportions. Some stage bands exist solely for the purpose of convenience in supplying special programs of community service with no special concern for the possibility of teaching either jazz style or improvisation. Other stage band programs function as true "jazz lab" ensembles, exploring every avenue of this medium in music.

TRADITIONAL PROBLEMS OF IMAGE IN THE PUBLIC SCHOOLS

The problems of the acceptance of jazz in the schools gave birth to the title "stage" band, instead of "jazz" band. This renaming was a simple concession to the conservative tradition of the school and community which associated anything entitled "jazz" with its early and perhaps questionable environment. Perceptive band directors quickly learned they could dignify the efforts of this special ensemble by relating it to the theater, studio, or recording industry, thus taking it away from the "sinful" influences of a traditional "nightclub."

Such a designation relieved the concerns of legitimacy in the minds of the school and church community, but there was yet another barrier against the development of the true jazz programs which has not been entirely surmounted. In this case, the barrier exists in the minds of band directors who choose to limit their involvement in stage band for other reasons. These reasons may include a lack of skill and experience in the field, a prior "bad" experience either as a director or participant, or a simple lack of time, interest, and concern for this unique segment of musical experience.

Despite any negative connotations attached to the stage band, it has grown into a valuable and legitimate facet of the instrumental-music program in many parts of the country. The stage band permits the teaching of skills that are a vital segment of the arts in America and that have viable applications, both avocationally and professionally. When correctly conceived and taught, the stage band program fits well within the philosophy of cultural enrichment and community service. It is an art which expands both the musical skills and knowledge of performer and listener alike, and can be a legitimate and worthwhile goal of the total instrumental-music program.

SPECIFIC TEACHING OBJECTIVES

There is certainly nothing wrong with the stage band program that originates for the purpose of providing community service with an ensemble that has easy mobility and usually enjoys considerable popularity. This ensemble can be a valuable resource in the field of popular music. Such a program can achieve many of the objectives listed below; it may also serve as a beginning for a much more extensive program of jazz education that also satisfies the needs of community service. Objectives may include:

1. The expansion of performance opportunities for individual students in a different medium and style, one that may relate to the public more effectively than either the concert or marching band.

2. Provisions for learning new playing techniques in the control of dynamic ranges and expansion of registers.

3. The learning of new skills in articulation, interpretation, and phrasing.

4. The continued reinforcement of basic playing skills and expansion of sight-reading ability.

5. Improvement of confidence and self-reliance in the concept of "one-on-a-part" ensemble performance, much like the wind ensemble and symphony orchestra wind section.

6. The provision for additional opportunities for advanced instrumentalists whose progress is often retarded in school groups of average (or below) ability.

7. The provision of a laboratory and forum for learning jazz, including supervised listening, study of theory for improvisation, and experimental performance.

GUIDELINES FOR ORGANIZATION

The Schedule

The stage band, like any other phase of music instruction, should be scheduled as a part of the school day. In smaller school systems, scheduling may be a limiting factor that could preempt other teaching activities deemed more essential, or it could eliminate likely student candidates from participation because of schedule conflicts. If such is the case, it would be well to consider a period of time available before or after school, or during the lunch period. Weekly evening meetings are also a possibility when other times are not available. Stage band programs can exist quite successfully when meeting only during the second semester of the school term after marching season. Admittedly, a limited rehearsal schedule would also limit the emphasis and results of such a program, but it would satisfy a need and show good results under proper management.

Under ideal circumstances, stage band should be a part of the school day. If the full-band rehearsal takes place first period or during the morning, the last period of the day is usually good for the stage band. This period is generally flexible for students since it corresponds with the athletic period, and it offers the potential of extending past the school day when necessary. This option proves helpful when moving to or setting up for an evening performance.

Selecting Personnel

A call for auditions for stage band personnel will usually appeal to the more-talented and advanced students if they understand the function and mission of the group. A shortage of saxes can often be remedied by some help and encouragement to clarinet players who find the prospect of learning a second instrument to be an interesting challenge. The selection of a set drummer may be determined by the student who already owns a set of drums (sometimes necessitating the inclusion of more than one student who is already equipped with a trap set). In the event that none of the drummers owns a set, a limited expenditure for at least a bass drum pedal and a high-hat with cymbals to be used with existing equipment would be required in order to get started.

The selection of the remainder of the rhythm section may also depend upon the private ownership of electronic equipment. The acoustic (nonelectric) string bass is quite functional when equipped with an amplifying pickup and is easy to learn by a willing tuba player. The availability of an electric bass guitar player, even outside the band organization, is also common.

Piano keyboard personnel are usually in good supply, although again, such a student may have to be discovered from the nonband student body. The traditional upright or grand piano serves the stage band quite well, but an electronic piano has several advantages. First of all, the tuning of the electric instrument will remain constant. The trauma of tuning the winds to a seldom-used church piano a half-step low for a performance can be avoided. Most serious stage band programs eventually acquire an electric piano as well as a good public-address amplification system and related equipment. In building such an inventory of equipment, it is well to seek the advice of a music dealer and to observe the needs of an established program.

Initial recruiting efforts that do not at first produce a full and balanced ensemble need not be doomed to failure. Groups as small as six or eight players can produce satisfying results. Such a group might be made up of piano, trap set, two trumpets, three saxes, and one trombone. Arrangements providing for flexibility of instrumentation are available and can serve to get a beginning group started.

Selecting Music and Building a Library

A large selection of standard and special stage band charts is available in every style and difficulty level. The director without prior stage band experience and a limited budget should start with 10 or 12 carefully selected pieces in a reasonable difficulty range. These arrangements should be charts which could serve to make up a performance of approximately an hour, thereby providing for the possibility of a first appearance. The advice of a trusted music dealer or friend in the profession would be a necessity. Under certain conditions a dealer might permit the music to be taken out "on approval" with return privileges of a certain portion of the order.

The process of building a stage band library must take into account the immediate and long-range objectives of the program. The goals of both performance and teaching would mandate the inclusion of standard materials in both rock and jazz idioms. Along with these staples should be a smaller supply of popular tunes that require less-intense study and serve for the enjoyment of the ensemble and its audience.

The legacy of the big bands can require a substantial investment in both the library and curriculum of the stage band. Teaching the ensemble structure and style of groups like Count Basie, Duke Ellington, Woody Herman, Les Brown, and Tommy Dorsey, to name but a few, has an important role in the mission. Equally as important would be that effort devoted to understanding the rock style as illustrated by groups such as Dick Grove, Jamey Aebersold, Thad Jones, and Chuck Mangione. In addition to teaching interpretation of ensemble sound, solo and improvisational techniques must be included in any serious effort of jazz study. Teaching these skills would require textbook materials, some of which are listed at the end of this chapter.

In addition to a regular library of stage band charts and study materials, serious planning for listening to recorded examples of good jazz and rock should be done. Most band rehearsal rooms include adequate playback facilities, but all too often any recordings of this type come from the private holdings of the band director. Unfortunately this may be the best and only source for hearing jazz groups of the past, but students should be afforded supervised listening experience of quality performances. Students may also be encouraged to share their own recordings with the class in support of certain objectives. Regular listening sessions of short duration (10 minutes or less) should be scheduled once or twice weekly for stage bands that meet a daily schedule. Such listening is especially important when learning improvisational skills.

The Stage Band Rehearsal

One of the most relevant problems in developing the stage band lies in the management of a structured rehearsal environment without suppressing the freedom which underlies the correct feeling for jazz and stage band work. The freedom and relaxation which is inherent in a good performance is generally foreign to the approach used with either the concert or the marching band. Both of these groups are built upon reaction to a disciplined and highly structured base. The student studying improvisation becomes completely independent from the control of the director when working toward objectives of originality. Yet, the confines of the chorus and chord structure underlying all jazz-solo performance must be observed, and should continue to be the controlling factor. The general concept of articulation is vastly different from that required in the concert band, with constant emphasis on relaxation and legato syllables in tonguing. The temptation for immature players to confuse the styles and let relaxed interpretation turn into undisciplined performance is a common occurrence. Converting and maturing student attitudes requires skill and vigilance from the director.

The stage band rehearsal must have the same components of the rehearsal found in the companion full-band rehearsals. The rehearsal should include warm-up and tuning exercises in preparation for the main body of the rehearsal, during which the concentrated study of one or more pieces takes place. The rehearsal should end with a "performance-reading" of music previously studied or prepared. A major difference of the stage band rehearsal would be in the nature and extent of the warm-up and tuning segments. The warm-up should not require as much time as the full band for two reasons: (1) The stage band rehearsal would not be the first time in the day that students play their instruments, assuming that a full band rehearsal precedes the stage band period; and (2) the stage band is a smaller group and need not include the accompanying instructional features of a full band warm-up. Tuning should be accomplished quickly by individuals and rechecked during the rehearsal on signal from lead players. The usual full-band procedure of unison "scale-tuning" should not be as necessary for students of this level of advancement. However on occasion, all groups, and especially those students doubling on second instruments, should be afforded the listening opportunity of playing complete scales. Brasses should also have the opportunity to check scale-tuning at expanded dynamic extremes. This kind of tuning helps students recognize how pitches center differently at contrasting dynamic levels.

THE CURRICULUM AND GOALS

Performance

The curriculum of the stage band is generally more performance-oriented than the full band; that is, the goal of the stage band is *not* primarily that of learning to play the instrument and achieving a basic ensemble character. The stage band is intended, instead, to take the skills achieved in full-band experience and expand them into a new medium. Thus the emphasis is to learn new techniques, and in the process, enlarge upon the register, dynamic range, and interpretive understanding of a new musical form.

In this process, the student is isolated on a part for which he is solely responsible and must now learn to fit into the harmony and balance of the ensemble. He learns to depend largely upon his *hearing,* rather than his *sight,* for the achievement of this goal. It is true that the kinds of ensemble sounds are reduced to only brass and saxophone and their combinations, but the placement is always dictated by a controlling rhythmic feeling rather than the conducted pulse.

Teaching Style

The unique series of articulated effects that result from written notation is no longer a mathematical value as in the equal subdivision of the beat when playing eighth notes. Instead, it becomes a series of judgments of *when* a note value must be altered and *what* value is reassigned to it for proper interpretation. For example, the pattern

in rock interpretation would sound;

while jazz phrasing would require it to sound;

This brief example opens the door to a comprehensive realm of problems in correct interpretation that should be solved as a first part of the curriculum. An excellent reference and teaching guide for this objective appears in the book *The Jazz Rock Ensemble* by Tom Ferguson and Sandy Feldstein. The chapter entitled "What Makes the Sound of Jazz and Rock" provides a comprehensive collection of examples in notation and their application to the two styles. This chapter is, of course, only a beginning, and a complete study of interpretation through notation is a major goal for the school stage band. The value of hearing good recorded style is most important as well as the regular experience of the performance of these styles.

This goal of learning the correct style and achieving the characteristic ensemble sound should be the first priority in the stage band curriculum. Since most young musicians are more familiar with the phrasing and interpretation of the rock style, they will identify and assimilate this idiom more easily. For that reason it serves as a more convenient starting point in the teaching and performing process. As the ensemble begins to feel comfortable with the rock sound, the director should add the study and performance of "big band" style, starting with Glenn Miller and progressing to Duke Ellington, Les Brown, and Woody Herman arrangements.

Teaching Improvisation

A second level of concentration in the stage band curriculum would include the study of improvisation. Although this skill can be approached with a beginning stage band, it seems better to give such a group time to develop some competence in developing sound and style before delving into the more academic area of improvisation. Since this skill is based on a fundamental understanding of the theory of music, it requires a more serious interest in intellectual study; a first requisite would be a complete knowledge of keys and scales. Most band programs include and emphasize such a theoretical foundation for all students, since scales are a normal requirement for any audition. This requirement should provide for a logical progression to chord structure which is paramount to improvisation. Students must become comfortable with the knowledge of transposition for their instruments, and preliminary efforts at teaching harmonic structure and transposition are most easily accomplished at the piano keyboard. Although it is usually impractical to expect all members of the stage band to gain keyboard proficiency, the more serious students will take advantage of every opportunity to learn basic harmonic progression such as the standard blues. It remains the responsibility of the director to maintain at least an elementary skill at the piano in order to demonstrate chord progressions.

BIBLIOGRAPHY

Aebersold, Jamey. *A New Approach to Jazz Improvisation* (32 volumes of play-along records). (New Albany, IN: J. A. Publications, 1967-1984)

Baker, David N. *Jazz Education for Teacher and Student.* (Bloomington, IN: Frangipani Press, 1981)

Brown, Ray. *Bass Method.* (Studio City, CA: First Place Music Publications, 1971)

Brown, Ray, and Steve Brown, *An Introduction to Jazz Improvisation* (book with accompanying record). (Los Angeles, CA: Creative World, 1973)

Burns, Roy. *Drum Set Artistry* (book with accompanying record). (Sherman Oaks, CA: Alfred Publishing Co., Inc., 1971)

Campbell, Gary, Jimmy Casale, Jerry Coker, and Jerry Greene. *Patterns for Jazz.* (Hialeah, FL Studio P/R, Inc., 1970)

Carubia, Mike. *The Sound of Improvisation* (with optional cassette). (Sherman Oaks, CA: Alfred Publishing Co., Inc., 1977)

Charlton, Andrew, and John DeVries. *Jazz and Commercial Arranging* (two volumes). (Englewood Cliffs, NJ: Prentice-Hall, Inc., 1982)

Coker, Jerry. *Improvising Jazz.* (Englewood Cliffs, NJ: Prentice-Hall, Inc., 1964)

Coker, Jerry. *The Jazz Idiom.* (Englewood Cliffs, NJ: Prentice-Hall, Inc., 1975)

Coker, Jerry. *Listening to Jazz.* (Englewood Cliffs, NJ: Prentice-Hall, Inc., 1981)

Feldstein, Saul, and Joe Scianni. *The Sound of Rock.* (Sherman Oaks, CA: Alfred Publishing Co., Inc., 1972)

Ferguson, Tom, and Sandy Feldstein. *Jazz-Rock Ensemble: A Conductor's & Teacher's Guide.* (Sherman Oaks, CA: Alfred Publishing Co., Inc., 1976)

Fink, Ron. *Drum Set Reading.* (Sherman Oaks, CA: Alfred Publishing Co., Inc., 1973)

Gridely, Marc C. *Jazz Styles.* (Englewood Cliffs, NJ: Prentice-Hall, Inc., 1978)

Grove, Dick. *Theory of Improvisation* (three volumes). (Studio City, CA: First Place Music Publications, 1975)

Henry, Robert E. *The Jazz Ensemble, A Guide to Technique.* (Englewood Cliffs, NJ: Prentice-Hall, Inc., 1981)

Lawn, Rick. *The Jazz Ensemble Director's Manual* (book with accompanying record). (Oskaloosa, IA: C. L. Brenhouse Company, 1981)

Mateson, Rich, and Jack Petersen. *The Art of Improvisation, Volumes 1 and 2.* (New York, NY: Music Minus One,1973)

Tirro, Frank. *Jazz: A History.* (New York, NY: W. W. Norton Company, 1977)

Wright, Rayburn. *Inside the Score.* (Delevan, NY: Kendor Music, Inc., 1982)

Jazz Band Music Publishers

Alfred Publishing Co., Inc., 15335 Morrison Street, Sherman Oaks, CA 91403.

Berklee Press, 1140 Boylston Street, Boston, MA 02215.

C. L. Barnhouse, Music Publishers, Oskaloosa, IA 52577.

J. A. Publications, 1211 Aebersold Drive, New Albany, IN 47150.

Kendor Music, Music Publishers, Delevan, NY 14042.

Studio P/R Inc., c/o Columbia Pictures Pub., P.O. Box 4340, Hialeah, FL 33014.

14

Outside Support:
The Band Parents Club

The most common means of financial support for the band program from outside the jurisdiction of the school is the band parents organization. Groups of this nature exist throughout the country under an assortment of titles such as "Band Boosters," "Parents for Music," "Band Auxiliary Club," and an occasional trick title like "Band Aids." A great majority of these organizations exist solely for the purpose of raising money to supplement the goals or activities of the band program. A number of the groups also include various kinds of services, such as chaperoning trips, driving equipment trucks, preparing concert publicity, and various social activities. When properly managed, these support groups are a valuable adjunct to the band program and have a variety of benefits which go beyond the mission of supplementing the band budget.

PURPOSE OF ORGANIZATION

The organization of any support group of band parents or other adults will profit from the definition of a clearly stated purpose.

Although the band director may not always initiate the formation of such a group, it should function with his sanction, if not explicit direction. Under these conditions, it should be understood exactly what the goals are, and generally how long it may take to achieve them. The success of any such venture hinges on the perception of whether or not a common need actually exists. Although regular meetings are required during certain periods, meeting without clear objectives is usually counterproductive. Few adults and hardly any band directors need extra meetings to attend. Band parents quickly lose momentum when objectives are vaguely stated or have been completed.

LEADERSHIP AND OFFICERS

The leadership of a support group should be vested in as few officers as effective administration will permit. Truly effective leaders whose time and effort can be made available are seldom in great supply. Leaders should be carefully chosen with a full understanding of, and enthusiasm for, the mission at hand. But limiting the actual number of elected or appointed officers is not intended to imply that others should not be generously involved. The exact opposite is true. Effective leadership will employ as many other parents and adults as possible, but it will be done by assigning specific people to specific tasks which suit their special skills and talents. The news director of a local TV station, for example, is too busy to accept an office in the band parents club, but he may gladly write a script with program notes and serve as announcer for the spring concert. The mother of a large family will make an excellent chairperson of the telephone committee and perform a valuable service to the organization while minding the children at home. Conscientious people often agree to well-defined and terminal tasks, but would not otherwise accept a general assignment.

The critical offices required for administration of a band-support organization can be limited to the following four positions:

1. President: A person whose motives for support of the band program are unquestioned. A person familiar with the business community is always helpful, but a newcomer with enthusiasm and diplomacy can be very effective. Office seekers with an axe to grind and individuals who tend to identify with controversial positions should be avoided. A

good supporter and friend of the school system is an asset to the organization. A few well-placed telephone inquiries to other members of the community before nominating a candidate can be a worthwhile precaution.

2. Secretary-Treasurer: A person who has demonstrated concern for accuracy of detail and fiscal responsibility. Occasionally such a person must be bondable. This is a time-consuming duty and requires an ability to maintain accurate records.

3. Publicity Chairperson: A person of proven reliability and skill in communications, both written and oral; must also be an "idea person." The mission of this officer often controls the success of the project and needs energy and enthusiasm to start and finish a project. Must understand the elements of a publicity campaign and be able to meet deadlines. Should develop a good relationship with news media and have good judgment in disseminating information, posters, handbills, etc. where people congregate.

4. Projects Chairperson: Another idea person. Should be able to turn plans into action in organizing the business and administration of each project adopted. Perceives what it takes to get the job done in terms of people, time, material, and effort; then proceeds to get it done.

These four positions can mean the success or failure of the organization. These people must work closely with the band director, and on occasion, with other school officials. While they may not always agree with the band director, they should work "in agreement" with his position.

DIRECTION AND CONTROL

Band-support groups which add to the responsibilities and work load of the band director are not as helpful as those that function independently toward the achievement of the predetermined goals; the more independently such groups function in fund raising and other projects, the more effective they become. It would be ideal if the band director could be completely isolated from such activities, but such isolation is seldom possible or even desirable. The director must remain sufficiently involved to monitor the policies and activities of the group. Fund raising also involves a certain amount of time and energy from the band students as well as the director, and it represents a critical area which should be carefully spelled out as a part of the fundamental policy of operation. The following concerns should be addressed with certain guidelines:

1. The total operation of the support organization must be approved by the school administration and function in agreement with school policies. Explanation of, and compliance with, school policy is usually the responsibility of the band director. He or she should take the initiative in keeping the principal and superintendent of schools fully informed of plans and activities, and solicit approval for any planned project. In some instances, certain projects may be presented to the superintendent or school board by the president of the group, but at no time should they be encouraged to pursue a course of action or a project which does not have the full approval of school authorities. These instances would include the following:
   a. Fund raising for band travel. Fund raising can be anytning from a picnic at the end of the year in a local recreation area to a trip by air to a foreign country.
   b. Fund raising for uniforms or equipment. This activity as either an independent project or cooperative funding with the school.
   c. Projected methods of fund raising including direct solicitation, advertising sales, ticket sales for breakfasts, dinners, bingo games, carnivals, selling chances on a boat or automobile, selling items of any kind, and also various promotions to receive money from the community in any other way.

2. Limitation of demands placed upon the time and effort of both director and students. The director of bands normally has a full-time position and whatever may be required of him or her in additional time and effort must have limits. Any project involving band travel and participation has a built-in requirement for extra time in preparation. The director should be allowed to devote his energies toward that objective.

   The students in the band program are more often exploited in fund raising than anyone else. There should be clear limits on their participation in matters of solicitation and selling. Many band directors prefer to exempt students from such activities while others limit their participation to one or two direct-sales campaigns.

PROJECTS AND ACTIVITIES

The list of activities which booster groups may choose to support include every item of funding a band program may require. The support may also be in terms of service in various activities, performances, and travel which are included in any normal band program. Here are some typical examples:

1. Funded Support:
   a. Band uniforms or special attire: rainwear, cold weather protection, outdoor heaters, costumes.
   b. Band equipment: instruments, special percussion equipment, electronic and sound equipment, recording and playback machines, stage band fronts, risers.
   c. Office machines and equipment: furniture, copying and duplicating machines, word processors: computers with programs for charting marching maneuvers, library catalogue, uniform and equipment inventory, as well as budget control and management.
   d. Band travel: charter bus service; funds for food and lodging and other travel costs. This kind of support is usually organized as a specific project—World's Fair Trip, Rose Bowl Parade, International Competition—or simply a trip and performance at an entertainment park in a neighboring state. Such travel sometimes requires approval of a state controlling agency.

2. Service Support:
   a. Providing drivers for equipment truck or bus travel.
   b. Providing chaperones or sponsors for routine band travel to contest or school athletic events.
   c. Providing labor, skills, and material for projects such as lighting of marching-practice area, or building an observation platform for marching rehearsal. Completion, renovation, or expansion of rehearsal, office, storage, or library

facilities. Building props, podiums, and seating for outdoor performance. A "shell raising" in the park for summer concerts.

d. Providing ushers for concerts and distribution of programs. Lending assistance with public address, risers, or other physical setups. Providing assistance with student control in performances which involve beginners or several bands. Preparing special stage props or scenery.

e. Food service at special summer camps or enroute to performance or on tour.

The preceding examples of useful support can be developed from band parents and other interested adults. Such assistance has great value to the success of the band program, and can serve to unite a community in a more fundamental philosophical manner as they become actual participants in a successful music-education program. This assistance serves to bring adults in the community much closer to the basic problems in education, helping to foster a mutual concern for the solution to these problems. This involvement gives adults a much clearer perception of the values of a band program and it can be a positive force in achieving the true musical goals as they witness the results of combining their own, perhaps common, physical efforts with that of the music specialist.

WAYS AND MEANS

Identifying Needs

Once the organizational groundwork of the support group has been accomplished with officers elected or appointed, it is time to survey the mission. This mission is the responsibility of the band director in consultation with his principal, and it should take place in conjunction with approval of the band budget whenever possible. The feeling of mutual cooperation between school and community is fostered when the band director can outline the year's goals with a clear statement of the level of financial support anticipated from the school. The act of informing the support group of what funding or services will first be pledged by the school serves to foster a partnership in the support of worthwhile educational projects. By personally appearing to make such information available, the school principal or superintendent can demonstrate his support for the band program and at the same time encourage outside support with his sanction. After such a presentation by the school official, the band director might capsulize his goals and request for support, using the sample shown in Figure 14-1.

	Central Public School Bands Projected Goals: 19__ Year		
Item	Estimated Cost	Budgeted by School	Needed from Boosters
UNIFORM/EQUIPMENT ADDITIONS			
100 hats and blouses w/sash	$ 6,000	$ 3,500	$ 2,500
20 flags and pikes	1,000	0	1,000
INSTRUMENT ADDITIONS			
1 English horn, 1 bassoon, 2 bass clarinets. Total:	4,300	3,000	1,300
TRAVEL			
6 trips, school athletic events:	6,800	6,800	0
3 trips, band contest/festival:	2,200	2,200	0
International Festival, Montreal:	22,500	0	22,500
Totals	$42,800 −	$15,500 =	$27,300

Figure 14–1   Request for funded support.

During the presentation of these funding goals, the representative school official might choose to fully explain his position and his endorsement of the request, and present a clear picture of other costs of the band program and how they are being met. The band director must be able to answer detailed questions that might come up regarding specific items.

Approving and Adopting the Needs

In the normal business routine of the parents organization, the President would then ask for adoption or approval of the request for funding. The ensuing discussion and vote of the membership would then give the band director a clear indication of how to proceed with his future planning. Final approval could take the form of endorsement of the total request, an altered or amended endorsement, or a rejection of the entire amount.

Once the level of support by the Booster group is official, it becomes the responsibility of the president to set in motion a plan to raise the funds approved by the membership. He could elicit suggestions from the group, school officials, and the band director about specific projects which could best achieve the goals. Such plans must always fit into the calendar of school and community events, and finalization of the planning includes setting certain dates. These tasks can be accomplished with the assistance of the school official in attendance.

Planning Projects

The selection of projects for fund raising can best be completed by an "executive committee" of the officers. The projects would then be presented to the entire organization at the next meeting for approval. Such an agenda item might look like Figure 14-2.

The projects shown are fairly common throughout the country and have proven successful in many communities. Exactly how an organization chooses to proceed in raising money within the community should be carefully planned. The members of the organization are in a better position to assist in making certain judgments of project effect and effectiveness. For example, organizations should not elect to sell a product or service in direct competition with local businesses.

Getting On With the Job

The organizational procedure now turns to the Projects Chairman for action that will hopefully convert the plan into results. This officer must carefully assess the needs of each individual project with the expertise to appoint or select an effective person to be in charge of each one. For example, the organization of concession sales at the home football games has been done by a person with a history of success. There is no reason to change: She knows exactly who can and will help, and she also knows *how* to get the job done. The community birthday calendar project is a different problem; it was tried last year and after payment of the bills, showed a profit of only $12.72. Much of

Band Boosters' Club
Central Public School Bands
Projects Report: 19__ Fiscal Year

The following fund-raising projects are recommended for support of the
Central Public School Bands:

Project	Anticipated Income		Total Need
OPERATION OF CONCESSION STAND			$27,300
6 Home Football games		$ 4,800	Bal: 22,500
COMMUNITY BIRTHDAY CALENDAR			
Listings and sales	1,800		
Advertising sales	1,200	3,000	Bal: 19,500
GENERAL FOOD SALE DAY*		7,300	Bal: 12,200
STUDENT SALE OF SELECTED ITEMS			
Participation of all band students in city-wide campaign		6,800	Bal: 5,400
SPRING BENEFIT CONCERT			
Ticket Sales	1,200		
Program Advertising	3,800		
Concessions	500	5,500	Excess over goal: 100

*Participating retail grocery and fast-food outlets contribute a percent of gross sales
on designated "Band Benefit Day."

Figure 14–2   Sample agenda item.

this work can be done by telephone—soliciting and collecting birthday information. By keeping the advertising cost low and allocating less space to each ad, more advertisements can be sold, thereby improving the profits. There is a "right" person to administer this project—one who relates well over the telephone, but must, because of family or health, spend much time at home. Such a person may need help in getting material to the printer and deliveries made, but she is devoted to the mission and the project will be completed.

Administrative Control and Guidance

Each project must be planned and coordinated with skill and discrimination. The promotion of one must not conflict with another, and the community must remain informed and reminded about the goals, their worth, and the outcome of the projects.

The band director continues all the while to monitor and encourage these efforts, while maintaining his position as the music authority, and relating the musical goals to the means. He may occasionally be invited to function as a mediator of major or minor differences of opinion that arise among the adults, but the conflicts should remain a responsibility of the leadership within the support group. Every effort should be made to maintain his authority in musical matters without becoming embroiled in problems between other adults.

Retail Business Support—Food Sales

"General Food Sale Days" have grown in popularity. These projects involve the promotion of local business establishments who agree to contribute a certain portion of sales or receipts on a specified day or period of time. These sales open up a variety of both private and corporate business in any community The impact of a well-advertised campaign for a specific cause normally generates an abnormal increase in business volume that also proves to be profitable for the participating firm. Grocery stores who agree to such a proposal can choose their traditional low-sales day of the month and double or even triple their volume on a special "Band Benefit Day." The increased volume along with the tax benefit of charitable contributions makes it worthwhile for everyone involved. Such projects meet several other important criteria for fund raising: The recipient or benefiting organization has no inventory investment; there is nothing to spoil or send back if it is not sold, and the profits are retained within the community, thereby eliminating any resentment against outsiders who might benefit from the program.

The "General Food Sale Day" is an important approach to fund raising. This project needs the leadership of a person in the business community who can talk to other business men and women, that is, someone who understands the regulations and policies of private and corporate business. The logical person may well be the president of the booster club who is a franchise owner of a fast-food outlet as well as an active member of the Chamber of Commerce. The sale can become his special project, involving not only his own business, but that of others like him. He will work carefully with the club Publicity Chairman. Once the participants are identified and committed, the word must spread through local newspaper, radio, and television media. On the day of the event, a group of volunteer students may need to distribute handbills. The organization and timing of this project over a ten-day period will be important to a successful conclusion.

Index